WOLF TREE

AN ECOPSYCHOLOGICAL MEMOIR IN ESSAYS

WOLF TREE

HEATHER DURHAM

HOMEBOUND PUBLICATIONS
WWW.HOMEBOUNDPUBLICATIONS.COM

HOMEBOUND PUBLICATIONS

WWW.HOMEBOUNDPUBLICATIONS.COM

Homebound Publications is a registered trademark of Homebound Publications

© 2022 TEXT BY HEATHER DURHAM

Homebound Publications supports copyright. Copyright fuels creativity, encourages diverse voices, promotes free speech, and creates a vibrant culture. Thank you for buying an authorized edition of this book and for complying with copyright laws by not reproducing, scanning, or distributing any part of it in any form without permission. You are supporting writers and allowing Homebound Publications to continue to publish books for every reader.

The author has tried to recreate events, locales and conversations from her memories of them. In order to maintain their anonymity in some instances she has changed the names of individuals and places, she may have changed some identifying characteristics and details such as physical properties, occupations and places of residence.

All Rights Reserved
Published in 2022 by Homebound Publications
Cover Design and Interior Design by Leslie M. Browning
PBK 978-1-953340-42-9
EBOOK 978-1-953340-51-1
Cover Image © Alfons Taekema
Interior Images by © Lisla

10 9 8 7 6 5 4 3 2 1

Look for our titles in paperback, ebook, and audiobook wherever books are sold. Wholesale offerings for retailers available through Ingram. Homebound Publications & Divisions is distributed by Publisher's Group West.

Homebound Publications, is committed to ecological stewardship. We greatly value the natural environment and invest in environmental conservation. For each book purchased in our online store we plant one tree.

TABLE OF CONTENTS

PART I — PSYCHOLOGY: FIRE & WATER

- 1   The Fall
- 7   Primary Relativity
- 13   Farm Animals
- 23   Little Lights
- 37   Better Than Dolphins
- 43   Baptisms
- 51   Ablaze
- 55   Speed
- 67   Undertow
- 85   Dismembering
- 89   Fractions
- 95   Journaling Purgatory
- 107 Pilgrim
- 121 Ergo Sum
- 141 Side Effects

PART 2 — ECOLOGY: ANIMAL & EARTH

- 151 Outside This Skin
- 167 To Remain Silent
- 183 Free Hands
- 193 Grimm's Ducklings
- 199 Elvis Lives
- 207 Menu
- 217 Alarming
- 229 Thy Neighbor as Thyself
- 255 Them
- 265 Alone Together
- 275 The Great Divide
- 283 Licorice Ferns in Winter
- 291 Lone Wolf
- 307 Fairy Tale

Acknowledgements

End Notes

PART I: PSYCHOLOGY

Fire & Water

The Fall

DAD

BAREFOOT IN BLUE JEAN OVERALLS, you pulled Dad's green felt sun hat over your freckled ears and followed him outside. Off the back stoop of your lemon-yellow house with the goldenrod shutters nestled an elfin woodland you explored together. The outside world held secrets, and your father knew them.

Wintergreen grows under the pine trees. Look for the red berries; they taste better than the lifesavers. Did you know you can eat violets? They taste like honey. And nasturtiums? They taste like black pepper.

Milkweed seeds are soft as silk against your cheeks, but be careful; the sap is poisonous.

HORSE

Beyond the trees, a slatted wooden fence hugged a wild pasture where horses frolicked. You gazed at them for hours. Listened to them munching hay, a rhythmic open-mouthed chomping with big yellow teeth. Sometimes when one came to visit, you reached up to let his fuzzy chin hairs tickle your cupped hand.

UH-OH

Before you uttered your third word, *horsie*, or your second, *DaDa*, one day you pushed your food off your highchair and announced, uh-oh! The revelation of something once present, now gone.

DAD

With strong, calloused hands, Dad crafted magic in the garden. Tomatoes, squashes, corn, beans, and peas sprouted from the dirt. Under the dirt was where the carrots lived, crunchier and sweeter than any that came from the store. From fragrant dill and warty cucumbers, you helped make pickles.

Medicine grew in the garden, too. Rub tansy leaves on your skin to keep away mosquitoes. Pennyroyal also works. Peppermint is good for bellyaches, and you can nibble it right off the stem.

Crouching barefoot in his overalls, red beard pointing at the earth and eyes twinkling like a leprechaun, Dad plucked a round stem of purple-flowering grass and crunched it between his teeth.

HORSE

Horses spend all day eating, running in the field, and sleeping standing up. You wondered if they got bored since they couldn't splash in a kiddie pool, ride crooked pink bikes on training wheels up and down the driveway, or don bathing suits and dance with Mom and Dad in a warm summer rain. Then again, horses don't argue and never yell or cry, so maybe it would be nice to be a horse.

UH-OH

Mom was crying again. You stood next to where she sat on the faded yellow couch, hugged her thin waist, smoothed her long blond hair against her orange collared shirt and told her, *It's okay Mom; I'll make you happy.* But you couldn't.

A new ache seeped into your stomach like a milky white poison. Peppermint wouldn't help. You knew something was changing, but you were powerless to stop it. You felt the anticipation of something precious about to slip off a precipice, away from you.

DAD

Dad was shouting again. Muscled arms taut, fists clenched, his face an overripe tomato, he side-kicked the broken dishwasher. Then a front-kick, the china cabinet shuddering from across the room. He stomped down the basement stairs, slammed the door. Still shouting. Cursing the neighbors' barking dog, his oppressive job, the evil government, his heartless father, and Mom.

Maybe he had milkweed in his belly too.

HORSE

You started grinding your teeth at night. The nails-on-a-chalkboard squeaking, clacking, and gnashing wasn't anything like horses munching hay. Sometimes it woke your baby sister. Usually, though, she slept through it, just as she slept through all the shouting, crying, and crashing down the hall.

You also began to sleepwalk. Sometimes just into the hallway, sometimes into Mom and Dad's room, and one time, you almost made it outside.

UH-OH

You were punching both fists against the glass door because you couldn't reach the handle and Mom was on the phone not listening to you and you banged and you banged because you needed the door opened NOW. The sour ache in your stomach.

The door shattered. Everywhere, glass and blood and screaming. A gash from wrist to elbow.

DAD

Dad was leaving. They said it wasn't your fault. And though you watched him pack up and drive away, you kept hoping he would come home. He never did.

Soon you too would have to leave your garden and your woods and the horses. Your peppermint and violets and milkweed. All the tastes, smells, sights, sounds, and sensations that meant Home.

You'd stomp your feet, clench your fists around the straps of your overalls and rage at your mother, your little sister, and the whole confusing world. For weeks and months and years, you'd kick broken toys, slam bedroom doors, and curse heartless kids. The neighbors' barking dogs, oppressive jobs, the evil government, and toxic relationships. Just like him.

HORSE

One day as you squat on muscled legs, barefoot in an elfin woodland, you will pull a green sun hat over freckled ears, nibble the acerbic tang of clover-shaped wood sorrel and remember the first place. The warm rain on your skin, the sweetness of wintergreen berries, the musk of the horses. The very earth that held you, taught you, nourished you, and was taken from beneath you. And you will begin to wonder if maybe, all along, that was the loss that mattered most.

Primary Relativity

I: GEOMETRY

I thought it would be shaped like a star, but Star Island was round. A round rock in the round ocean encircled by the round horizon. Standing on that island surrounded by ocean and sky, I should have felt at the center of everything. Instead, I felt stretched, felt a line connecting me west to the mainland, back to the familiar shapes of my Massachusetts home—the rectangular house with the square lawn, vegetable garden in equidistant rows, patchwork woodland, and all the empty spaces that no longer held my father after he'd driven away north. And once we loaded the box of our moving truck and drove away south, it no longer held us.

I found no right angles on Star Island. The ground undulated with boulders and odd outcroppings of sedge and shrub in the areas where soil wedged in cracks in the rock. The aging grand hotel with the crooked shutters and warped porches seemed to list to one side like a marooned oceanliner. Beyond the hotel, seventeenth-century stone cottages rested at odd angles amidst jagged rocks like a New England cemetery.

I gazed across patches of thistley grass past the cottages to the stone chapel where my mother was communing with other single mothers. Then angled to the left to spot my little sister with her daycare group playing in one of the gazebos. The lines that connected us now formed a lopsided triangle. We were still getting used to that shape.

I stood apart from the older kids' group on the rocks near the water. Our counselors, glistening in baby oil, lounged on garish beach towels and whispered as loud as speaking about the cute boy working in the kitchen. For once, I didn't feel like eavesdropping. I turned away from the land and watched the sky.

The sky was so much bigger on the island than back in Massachusetts or Connecticut. Back there, you could always see houses and trees and hills with more trees but Star was enveloped in water and sky. If I squinted, I could find the faraway point where the water ended and sky began and follow its arc all the way over to the water on my opposite side. Not the solid arc of a frown, but diffuse, infinite, a deep breath inhaled and exhaled. The arc of a new question still taking shape.

II: GRAVITY

I stood at the point where rock met sea. Saltwater lapped at my blue water sneakers, seeped in cold to where my toes scrunched rubber against rock. Just beyond my toes, the inky water roiled and frothed, a cold boil concealing thick mats of kelp and those green jeweled sea vegetables we'd tasted on our morning adventure. I scratched at a flake of skin peeling off my sunburned nose, tightened my ponytail that was more like a tangled mat of salted seaweed, pulled the elastic from my bathing suit lower on my legs, and squatted down to look in the water.

I tried to see in, to see through, but I couldn't. I wondered how far to the bottom. Maybe it went down to the center of the earth. Maybe that was so much farther than I'd thought. How far away was my father? Was my sister okay? When would my mother be done with her meeting? Would she have cried today and try to hide it? How could I make it better? The lines connecting me to all of them throbbed in my chest like burns. I returned my attention to the rock beneath me.

A vein of glassy mica caught my eye and I leaned forward to pick at it, to pull it from the rock so I could take it with me. Mica was my favorite part of Star Island; there was a lot of it in all that granite. Most of it was silver, but my favorite was black mica. Still shiny but dark and mysterious. Less like discarded flakes of the counselors' nail polish and more like the ocean. I worked at it with fingernails grown long and pulled up a nice thick chunk of the mineral, one with several layers that I would enjoy peeling apart, one by one.

Then, a wave crashed down on the rocks, on me. I sucked in air and reveled in the shocking coolness, the freshness that seemed to wake me up and wipe me clean in an instant.

I blinked as saltwater dribbled down my face and into my mouth. I exhaled.

III: ENTROPY

Grasshoppers droned like Buddhist chanting in the puritan village. Sailboat riggings chimed against masts. The breeze tossed my salt-matted hair up. A few feet out, ripples broke the surface of the chop, an upside-down splash. A school of fish swarmed like bees, then sunk into the murky deep.

I turned around, saw the other kids still playing, counselors still talking. I turned back to the water. The wave had washed the mica from my hand, and I watched it floating on the surface of the ocean, a tiny black window. I hugged my arms around my knees and leaned forward.

Sharks lurked under there. Currents shifted and swirled. Fathers left. Mothers packed you up and moved you away from everything you knew. Boxes and rooms and houses couldn't contain anything. Skies expanded. Stars floated in the ocean. The ocean contained depths I would never know. I was just a speck on the surface.

How might it feel, *not* to be tethered to any of it?

I closed my eyes, held my breath, and dove in.

Farm Animals

I tossed my bookbag to the floor of the school bus and collapsed on the black vinyl bench seat. "We just walked a whole mile," I announced to my seatmate, who eyed the other farm kids shuffling down the aisle and nodded in polite sympathy.

I brushed a smear of dirt off my elbow and pulled a piece of hay from my shoe. I exhaled a long breath, leaned back against the seat, and watched the farm retreat as the bus sped away.

We didn't really mind the walk.

That mile-long pot-holed gravel road where no school bus would dare traverse wound its way among oaks, beeches, and sycamores to the humble pastures and weathered white barns of Auerbach 4-H Farm. "Auer Farm," to Connecticut locals. Our Farm, to us kids.

On the outskirts of suburban Bloomfield, just minutes from urban Hartford, Auer Farm's 120 rural acres sustained an apple orchard, corn and hay fields, a pumpkin patch, an herb garden, goats, sheep, and a small head of cattle. The food, milk, and wool stocked a farm store by the main road. What had once been a larger-scale working farm but wasn't yet the bustling nonprofit farm education center it would become, was in the 1980s the quiet home of one farm manager, his family, and a handful of non-farming tenants.

At the end of the road, in a verdant meadow perched eight identical white cottages formerly inhabited by farmworkers. The last one at the top of the hill by the sugar maple and the creaky splintered wooden see-saw was my house. Mine, my little sister Becca's, and my divorced mother Judi's. For six years sandwiched between stints in more traditional suburban digs with paved driveways and squared-off lawns, the six years between kindergarten and sixth grade, six fatherless years between father and stepfather, I was a farm kid.

On school days, Becca and I started the procession of children amassing like water droplets flowing to a creek. Mom shooed us out the white metal porch door, the little sister with long straight champagne blonde hair and porcelain skin and the big sister with flyaway strawberry blonde tangles and freckles, both with matching KangaROOS zipper pocket sneakers and Jansport backpacks.

Past the tire swing that made black marks on bare thighs, trying not to trip over any of our five semi-feral cats, we trotted down to the screened-in porch of the next cottage to pick up Lisa, a quiet, fawn-eyed girl Becca's age. Beyond the edge of the cornfield after the maintenance sheds stood the airy two-story farmhouse where three rowdy boys lived—Eric, Jonah, and Seth. We six were the only school-aged kids on the farm at the time, the only kids at the end of our long wild road.

When in school, of course, we separated into socially appropriate groupings, following unwritten rules like *never associate with the opposite sex* and *ignore your siblings*. At school, I was timid and shy and spent a lot of time watching the other kids to figure out how I should act.

On the farm, I didn't worry about any of that. Our pack of boisterous children contained two compatible cliques: the Big Kids and the little kids. Eric, a year older, Jonah, my age, and I were the Big Kids. Becca, Lisa, and Seth were the babies, the ones to lecture and protect from danger and occasionally to make screech by throwing earthworms down their shirts.

Together we scampered back down the driveway of the farmhouse, around the minty chamomiley rosemary herb garden island, and onto the dusty lane that snaked into the green distance toward our bus stop.

The best journeys never follow straight lines. Our winding road offered unlimited opportunities for adventure for those who knew where to look. As kids, we knew.

Electrified wire fences hummed alongside much of the road, enclosing the black and white milk cows in their brambled pastures. Electric fences are endlessly tantalizing to free-range children, and each day brought new challenges.

I dare you to touch it.

Touch it with a stick.

Touch it with your sneaker.

I bet you can't climb under it.

See how close you can get before you get zapped.

If none of the dares produced the desired effect, naturally we started pushing each other. Giggling, shrieking, grunting, snarling, panting, we scuffled. The little kids soon removed themselves from the action and watched from the sidelines as Eric, Jonah, and I fumbled closer to the hum.

I can still remember the first time my body contacted the jarring, teeth-chattering, hair-frazzling, buzzing wires. Grade school shock therapy. Stunned and whimpering, I rubbed my zinging shoulder.

That broke the spell. The boys—my pack brothers—turned sympathetic, picked up my bag, and patted me on the back. Becca took my hand in hers. Zen cows looked up from pink salt licks, chewed their cuds.

Back on the road, we broke into running again. We were always running, in part to keep from missing the bus with all our mandatory play stops along the way, but mostly from some innate drive shared by feral kids everywhere. We weren't running *from* or *to* anything; we were just running. Legs pumping on the rocky dirt, kicking up dust or mud or snow, we galloped as stallions.

Even better than running was riding bikes, which we did almost every day after school, not a safety helmet among us, in games of cops and robbers and cowboys and Indians. Good guys chased bad guys, and eventually bad guys went to jail. Jail was naturally the hay barn with the giant-sized sliding wooden doors.

Running and riding bikes on rocky dirt roads meant that I almost always sported skinned knees and elbows, which were as much a part of who I was as my eternally sunburned and peeling nose, multiplying freckles, and tangled hair. Lest you picture me as a typical tomboy, my standard outfit at the time was a green wrap-around skirt with red strawberries and yellow raspberries, pink t-shirt, dirty sneakers, dirt-encrusted polished nails, and a pink yarn ribbon around my ponytail.

A few minutes from the boys' house, a shady cobbled brook meandered through the cow pastures and under the road where it was spanned by a simple round culvert and concrete bridge. The bridge and the water enticed us even more than the electric fence, and welcomed such diversions as rock-skipping and spitting contests. The one contest in which I could not compete was the peeing contest, as I lacked the necessary boy parts.

We Big Kids lined up on the wide concrete railing facing the water—two skinny tan kids with pants at their knees and a freckled skirt-adorned kid squinting attentively straight ahead. Becca, Lisa, and Seth had to wait for us on the road.

"Put your hands next to your eyes and only look straight ahead. No peeking!" the alpha male Eric commanded, though he didn't need to. Who wanted to see their gross penises anyway?

My job was to be the judge of Eric and Jonah, and at that I was always fair and honest. Usually, one of them got the prize for distance, the other for length of time peeing. I didn't mind my position, nor did I feel I was lacking. I could run just as fast as either of them, and who cared about peeing standing up?

In winter, when the brook froze and it was too cold for peeing contests, we hurled stones at the ice. Metallic pings and reedy pongs reverberated until the satisfying *shunk* when one broke through. If we felt headstrong or cocky, we might exchange dares to test our weight on the ice, better yet to creep through the dark culvert under the road from one side to the other. All who failed this most perilous challenge had to slink soaked and shivering back home to dry clothes and an angry parent who would then have to drive us to the bus stop or worse, if we missed the bus, to school. After that happened, we stayed off the brook for at least a few days and contented ourselves with crunch-stomping the paper-thin white puddle ice in the road and bellowing at the cows to try to get them to do something interesting, which they never did.

Cows interested us only when they gave birth, which was wonderfully disgusting, full of rude noises and mysterious gushing liquids and blood like the horror movies I was not supposed to watch but sometimes did anyway at Dad's (*Don't tell your mother*). We knew from science class that it is pretty much the same when people have babies, and we all agreed that people are pretty gross too.

Sheep entertained us when they transformed from big fuzzy Stay Puft marshmallows on legs to shivering naked Muppets that seemed embarrassed to be out in public, and since we were not involved in the shearing process, the transition always took us by surprise. "The sheep forgot to get dressed today" never got old.

Auer Farm didn't have chickens anymore, but their absence created unique opportunities for us: a mildewed, leaning, vine-draped, two-story, bigger-than-my-house chicken coop. Adults wagged their fingers at us and warned: "Do not go in there; it is dangerous and not a place to play."

We went there all the time.

As soon as you pushed through the creaky door, the odor hit you—the musty, moldy chickenshit smell like a mixture of wet newspapers, wood shavings, and steamy compost. The place looked like a tornado hit, or worse, like the chickens had mysteriously disappeared along with the people who should have come back to clean up. We knew about mysterious disappearances from one of our older neighbors who watched *The Twilight Zone*. Gray windows were cracked, shattered, or missing, and face-catching spider webs, fluttering moths, and diving bats competed with scurrying mice to elicit squeals which I never allowed to escape *my* lips, no way.

The first time we crept in together, tense and arms touching, not quite holding hands. Around every corner was a creepy, spine-tingling discovery. Squeaking stairs with gaping holes in them we just had to climb, conveyor belts with chutes through the walls to looming rooms we just had to explore, and a second-floor doorway that opened into thin air that we just had to open to look down and wonder. We barely breathed or dared to speak inside, but leaving, we loped across the field, practically cartwheeling with the ecstasy of our bravery and the elation of our secret.

Fortunately, the chicken coop was on the hill at the end of the road, not on the way to the bus stop, or we would never have gotten to school.

The rest of the road after the brook crossing was just cows and electric fences all the way to the farm store, where the paved entry road looped around a handful of apple trees. We waited there for the bus.

In the trees.

Well-pruned apple trees pose no challenge for short arms and legs, and we each claimed our own. My tree, a gnarled little thing, curved around me and held me like a mother, a mother bearing ripe red fruit. I knew the twists and turns of that tree like my own skin, and I climbed her almost every day.

But sometimes, a stack of hay bales next to the farm store beckoned us to play King of the Mountain. The rule was to get up on top and yell, "I'm the king of the mountain!" until someone felt like running up and trying to push you off.

Most times, you reigned for mere seconds before you found yourself usurped and among the civilians again, but that didn't matter. King or alpha male, boy or girl, big or little kid or kid without a father, we were all farm kids.

Though our pack would disperse and we would eventually become adults of cities, towns, forests, or mountains, our farm taught us lessons for all places. How to inhabit our animal bodies. How to inhabit a landscape. And that even the most humble landscapes are vast and worth exploring. Miles and years from Auer Farm, that would stick with me as viscerally as the zing of the electric fence.

Standing tall on hay bales, dust-covered, and faces flushed from running, we were more fully alive, more fully at home in our world than we would get to be the rest of the day. When the yellow of the school bus appeared around the bend, we hopped down, brushed ourselves off, and lined up for school. We put ourselves away. But come 3:30 pm, we'd be back on our dusty dirt road, home on Our Farm.

Little Lights

Where are you from?

I never know how to answer that.

Five years in the region of my birthplace of Springfield, Massachusetts. Divorce. Six years on a rural farm in Bloomfield, Connecticut. Remarriage. Six years of manicured lawns and well-funded schools of Glastonbury, Connecticut.

A fourth thread woven between standard school years in conventional towns stitched me firmly into a rustic village in the deciduous woodlands of southern New Hampshire, where I spent the better part of ten summers at YMCA Camp Takodah.

Can you hear the bell chime? Not the shrill alarm peals of grade school compounds but a quaint ding-dong like a church bell. Softly at first, then louder and faster as the bell ringer leaned into the rhythm, pulling and releasing the knotted nylon cord. Between dings, the wooden frame creaked with the weight of the swinging iron bell, but you could only hear that from the nearby cluster of matching green cabins. The ringing echoed from the archery range to the dining hall, the ropes course to the waterfront.

Eleven a.m. on the middle Sunday of girls' camp, the bell's invitation was clear. Clean and dressed in our Sunday finest—blue or white camp t-shirts and shorts—we followed our counselors like ducklings through the woods and down the hill toward the chapel. Senior staff greeted us on the path at the entrance, whispering and shushing us by example into quieter versions of our free-range summer selves.

Though the mission of the YMCA is "to put Christian principles into practice through programs that build a healthy *spirit, mind,* and *body* for all," Takodah was not a religious camp. It was a secular generalist sleep-away camp where I swam in sun-warmed waters, played four-square and kickball on the fields, and hand-dipped candles in the arts & crafts cabin, "hobby nook." In the evenings, I acted in skits, roasted marshmallows, scratched mosquito bites, and listened to ghost stories. Mind and body were invigorated.

And spirit? Though I wouldn't have used that word at the time, I did understand that Takodah was more than a place to play, more than glorified recess. Camp life was comprised of tradition, of rituals. The customs that year after year were as comfortable and natural as brushing your teeth—morning flag-raising with the sun on our faces and evening taps sung under the stars to the music of crickets and frogs—a culture of place difficult to explain to kids back home.

Home: an echoing cathedral-ceilinged new house in a ChemLawn yard landscaped with haughty pink rhododendrons, slivered mulch, and pristine white stones, set tastefully apart from similar houses with similar landscaping, all with steep winding driveways and shiny cars backing out of garages and revving off to somewhere else.

Home: in the new house in the new town, a new man shared my mother's bed. A man we were supposed to start calling Dad because he was sensitive and needed to feel loved. He was so sensitive he would cry or yell if he got his feelings hurt, and we could never tell which one it was going to be. He got his feelings hurt often.

Home: sixth grade on a new school bus where the popular girl sized me up and told me I wasn't allowed to sit in the back of the bus with the cool kids. Salon-permed hair thick with Aqua-net, pastel Benetton sweater knotted around her shoulders, canvas Tretorn sneakers shining white, a child of country clubs and garden parties, she made sure I knew I didn't belong. Blinking back tears behind my thick glasses, I returned to the front of the bus. In an encounter that lasted no more than two minutes, my place in the social hierarchy was set in stone for the duration of grade school.

I knew that by most definitions, I had it good, better than most, and home wasn't a terrible place to be. But home was no longer comfortable and predictable. It was barely recognizable. No longer *home*. Not like Takodah.

In our cabin groups, we filed down the wood-chipped aisle and onto the locally milled pine or spruce log bench assigned to us. Youngest campers in front, oldest up the hill of the natural amphitheater. Hemlocks, beeches, and sugar maples were our walls on three sides, and we faced Cass Pond, more accurately an expansive lake lined with wild blueberries.

My first summer at Camp Takodah, I had been wary of the activity on the Sunday schedule called "chapel" because it sounded like church. My immediate family didn't go to church or celebrate the religious parts of any of the holidays unless you count the desktop crèche Becca and I amused ourselves with every December, which was more of a dollhouse for some kid named Jesus, his pet sheep, and camels, and a few men in dresses. Our liberal hippie parents didn't tell us there was no god, or that there was one. They let us figure it out for ourselves, and as a kid I didn't think much about it.

My only experiences of church were the few times my sister and I accompanied my grandparents on Easter. I thought some of the songs were pretty, but the organ hurt my ears and the people singing didn't seem very happy to be there. I was too young to understand much of what the sweating red-faced man in the robe ranted about, but it seemed to me that religion was like a strict school where you had to follow a lot of rules or else suffer eternal pain and sorrow, like that tearful, bleeding man strung up by his wrists.

Takodah chapel was nothing like that.

"Welcome to chapel," the waterfront director, "Kingfish," said. Tan, sun-bleached, crinkly-eyed and smiling, this soft-spoken man in a white staff t-shirt and blue shorts set the stage for our chapel service. There was no mention of God, scripture, or other religious references I wouldn't have recognized. Instead, Kingfish asked for a few moments of silence and called our attention to our surroundings. To the rippling waves jostling the pebbles of the lakeshore. The wind in the leafy green trees and the clinking of sailboat riggings moored just offshore. The warm sun on our skin. For several minutes, all three hundred or so of us kids, college student counselors, and a handful of older adult staff looked around and listened, the blue lake sparkling back at us. And though I hadn't yet heard of the practices of meditating, tuning in to senses, grounding, or centering, I did know that I felt...awake. And calm. Like the water.

Then commenced the program for the day. First, a group of nervously giggling pre-teens got up and took turns reading a story about a man flinging starfish back into the sea and how it made a difference to each individual starfish. A group of leaders-in-training went up to the front and sang James Taylor's *You've Got a Friend*[1], arms around each others' shoulders and swaying as they sang until the whole camp joined in arms and swayed along with them.

I sang along when I knew the words, linked arms and swayed when everyone else did, and listened to what was shared. But I also just stared out at the sailboats moving in the breeze. How the wind caught the fiberglass boats and spun them around the points where they were attached to buoys. A big gust could whip several boats around at once so that they pirouetted in unison, or sometimes one took a solo. The sunshine's shimmering ripples swirled among them, up to the rustic wooden lakefront lodge and around the quiet waterfront docks, where in just a few hours we'd be splashing and squealing and spinning in inner tubes.

Arms around my cabin-mates I swung my legs making tracks in the woodchips below. I felt happy and safe and part of something important, something that had as much to do with the words shared as with the dancing sailboats, something bigger than me. Something like community.

A nine-year-old stammered through a poem she wrote that only the first couple rows could hear but everyone smiled and nodded in encouragement anyway. A counselor read a story about a tree that gives everything he can to a small boy[2], and another read a story about a leaf that doesn't want to let go of his tree in autumn[3]. Finally, the program director, José, closed chapel with a guitar-led folk song about molding a child's heart with love and art.

Sentimental mush, you say? Absolutely. But you go there to that lakeside chapel and listen to the sincerity in those voices. Look into their eyes and know they believe every word and see if you don't get a little choked up yourself. (You can, you know. Takodah lives on. Some cultures exist outside of time.)

The mood continued into lunch. Sunday lunch was a special meal—roast beef, mashed potatoes, and fresh-baked bread that had us salivating long before we clomped up the wooden dining hall steps.

We sang songs as tables were cleared, as with all meals in the big airy hall. But Sunday lunch we sang only "Sunday songs." The usual boisterous chanting clapping songs were replaced with quiet songs, serious songs. Not the simple sappy friendship songs of chapel, but wise, worldly music.

Because so many girls returned year after year and sang the same songs, the majority of us seated at the round wooden tables knew every word. No books, no instruction necessary. Once a leader stood and started a song, three hundred voices joined in, some slipping into harmonies, in some of the most hauntingly beautiful singing I will ever hear. The majority were old folk songs in minor keys.

I'm just as restless as wind blowing westward
I can't stay in any one place for too long.
I'll love you today but I'll leave you tomorrow
by morning you'll know I am gone.[4]

or

Calves are easily bound and slaughtered,
never knowing the reasons why;
those who truly treasure freedom,
like the swallow must learn to fly.[5]

or

There's a web like a spider's web,
made of silk and light and shadow,
spun by the moon in my room at night.
It's a web made to catch a dream, hold it tight till I awaken,
as if to tell me, my dream is alright.[6]

If the words seem melancholy, the melodies were even more so. There was a common theme of loss and yearning in Sunday songs. Too dark for innocent young children? Perhaps, if there were any innocent young children present, the meanings didn't register, not really. For the rest of us, they seemed about right.

Joining a line of girls carrying trays of clinking ice cream dishes and spoons up to the serving board, singing about a calf with a mournful eye bound for market made us realize, even if only subconsciously, that maybe there was a sad and broken world out there, but there were also places of joy and healing. Weren't we lucky to be here?

Sunday songs were not about religion, but poetry. They were aching with all it means to be a feeling thinking human. Like the moment of silence at chapel, the poetry of our music got inside me, reminded me, *this world is beautiful and complicated; pay attention.*

Sunday wasn't the only ritual day at Camp Takodah. The final Friday night before Saturday departure the staff switched off the lights inside and out and led campers without flashlights down to lakeside Memorial Lodge for Candlelight ceremony.

As we filed into the log cabin lodge, piano music wafted over us. Classical or new-agey George Winston, it filled the summer breezy candle-lit hall and mingled with the whisperings of the lake outside. We were enchanted. Nobody need ask us to hush at Candlelight.

What followed resembled chapel, but all the songs, stories, and poems took on a different feel that night, the last night before we all headed home to lives of less certainty, to new school years ahead. Many girls cried, dabbing eyes with wads of toilet paper they brought in anticipation.

I didn't dread going home, exactly, but at Candlelight I was always suddenly terribly 'campsick'—the feeling that more than anything I just wanted to stay at camp forever. I always cried. Sailboats wind-chimed, bullfrogs bellowed, and I choked up with everything that would be missing from life at home: the comforting structure, the joyful rituals, the grounding attention to the natural world. The feeling of being part of a group who shared in all of it, like a family.

My own family felt more like a changeable collection of separate parts. My little sister—sometimes friend and sometimes foe. My mother—sometimes mama bear and sometimes wounded bird. My new stepfather—the stray dog who's been kicked one too many times and might turn on you any minute. My father—the stranger I visited every other weekend, then once a month, then not so much anymore.

I know that family is supposed to be the one place you belong, but something in me felt separate, foreign. A tiny sailboat attempting to navigate a stormy sea of ocean liners and pirate ships.

At the end of the lodge ceremony the camp director lit a small white candle that had been sealed onto a birch bark round—the last candle lit from the previous candlelight ceremony, whether a couple weeks or a year before. He used that candle to light others. Hundreds of others. As he began, he read the following poem, the same one read every year since the camp's founding in 1922:

> As we light our candles we share our dreams;
> With each new light new vision gleams,
> and in the purifying light
> our spirits reach a fairer height;
> And in our hearts we breathe a prayer—
> God bless Takodians everywhere.

One by one, the support staff, then oldest campers on down to the youngest moved up to the front of the building and were handed candles. Even the little eight-year-olds, wide-eyed with responsibility, reached for candles of their own. Then they followed the procession out into the night.

As each group left the lodge, they walked up to the ends of the previous groups lining the gravel path up the hill, so that everyone walked a path of lights. Smiling teary-eyed faces glowed in the darkness. Sometimes we stopped to hug a friend or counselor we saw along the way, taking care to keep flames away from bangs and ponytails, but mostly we looked into each other's eyes and grinned with our whole bodies. If candles flickered out, we lit them from our friends and continued on. We walked the path until it was our turn to step in line and watch the younger kids walk by us, eyebrows furrowed with the concentration of tending their own special flames.

Once the last group left the lodge, those in line along the path started up behind them, so that the original path greeters were now walking up the middle. Places reversed; the young lit the way for the old. And so we continued until we arrived in one of the large playfields, forming a giant circle.

After everyone arrived in our circle of light, we sang *This Little Light of Mine*. For years I thought this was just a camp song, not a song with gospel roots. Like the Sunday songs that I would be shocked to hear sometimes on folk radio programs. In our version of *Little Light*, there were a few words changed here and there to make it secular—with no mention of God, faith, or the devil.

To me the song was about us, our camp community, and all that we were individually and together. That little light, in my hand, was mine. They gave it to me and it was my job to take care of it.

Did I find religion at summer camp? Not exactly. I certainly did not find God, that father figure up in the sky somewhere. I wasn't so big on fathers, anyway.

What I found instead was a mosaic of trees and water, stillness and joyful noise, dancing sailboats and silly dives, sappy songs and sad songs, roast beef and wild blueberries, flames and tears. I cemented the foundation of a deep connection with the natural world that would at times look a lot like spirituality, and I planted seeds of belonging to a congregation of others who feel the same.

That is where I am from. Those are my lights.

As I held my candle in the darkness I looked out across the circle at all the other little fires, swaying in time with the music, until the song ended. Then, gathering into cabin groups our counselors led us quietly, eyes drooping and fingers covered in wax, back to our cabins, where we would sleep soundly until the bell chimed in the new morning.

Better Than Dolphins

She's going to tell me her secret.

She'd motioned for me to sit and though I tried to perch on the edge of the cot, the plasticized mattress sank and the springs squeaked like all the camp beds did. It seemed louder than usual because everybody else was off splashing in the slimy pea-green pond, playing tetherball, flirting with boys or buying frozen Snickers at the camp store. But Siobhan was staff on duty in the cabin area, so that's where I wanted to be.

She was nothing like any of the other eye-shadowed hair-sprayed boy-crazy counselors at 4-H Camp. Siobhan was serious and quiet, with a faraway look like she was listening to something only she could hear. She knew things; you could tell. Or maybe that was what everyone from Ireland looked like. But a few of the other girls said she told them something important, something special. Top secret. And she wouldn't tell just anyone.

Siobhan raked slender fingers through sun-bleached snarls then pulled the cascading mass around her shoulder as she bent to plug in the fan. It commenced a pleasant hum, like a distant lawnmower. I leaned in.

The oppressive humidity was right on target for July in Connecticut, and I wanted to ask what it was like in Ireland right now. More than that I wanted to ask why on earth she chose to spend the summer here by a fishless pond when she could be home swimming in the ocean with dolphins.

I scratched a mosquito bite on my knee, listened to a fly bouncing against the screen door, and stayed quiet. It was a welcome change from the noise of bubbly girls and show-off boys, the noise I knew I was supposed to join in but rarely knew how. Coed 4-H camp was less like the solace of the girls camp I attended and more like the noise of high school where I would soon be returning for sophomore year, four years into a new town and somehow still invisible.

And the noise at home I wasn't supposed to hear— the nighttime thunderous *Goddamnit Judi* and the weepy *Please Bob don't*, doors slammed and his car retreating. The still worse daytime silence, the unvoiced lie that everything was fine.

I saw through the lies. There were always clues.

The slight choking sound in my mother's voice, the waver in her smile. The pinch in my stepfather's forehead, the pallid knuckles of his clenched hand. The chemical stench of whiskey on his breath. The feeling in my stomach like I'm falling and don't know when I'll hit the ground.

Siobhan squinted turquoise eyes in the direction of squeals coming from the bathhouse, probably deciding if she needed to investigate. When the din quieted she folded muscled legs onto her sleeping bag and turned her electric gaze on me. My face immediately felt hot and I looked down, studied my fingernails.

"Would ya like to hear a story?"

Oh, that voice! Leprechaun voice? Fairy voice? No, deeper, richer. Like molasses poured over river stones. The voice of a wise woman.

Oh yes, please, tell me!

I nodded.

"Can you keep it a secret? From everyone, yeh? Little ones don't understand and older ones won't believe."

"Of course," I whispered.

"You've heard I swam with a dolphin? I had to swim there for a long while before he would even come close. I went every day."

I nodded, glancing at the newspaper clipping tacked above her bunk. A flash of blonde hair and a willowy hand on a shining gray fin in the cerulean sea. Now that's what color water should be.

"Well, I went at night too, sometimes, if the moon was bright. Then I could be alone with him, away from the crowds. Can you picture that, just me and my dolphin under the moon?"

I could.

"Well, one time, I waited and waited and the dolphin didn't come. That one time, something else came. The most beautiful, the most marvelous thing I have ever seen. She climbed up on a rock and let me see her, in the moonlight. Then she swam away, and I never saw her again."

I was staring back, now. Enthralled. Entranced. She studied my face.

"You know, you have magic in you. You pay attention. You know how to be quiet and listen, and that's magic. Most people don't know how to do that anymore. Don't lose that when you get older, ya hear me?"

I tried to speak but instead had to gulp back something sharp and warm in the back of my throat, something that spread to my chest and burned like a hot coal. But in a good way.

I nodded, again.

"It was a mermaid."

I stared hard. Narrowed my eyes and studied her face. Her body. Looked closely for evidence of the lie. Her forehead—unwrinkled; her mouth—soft; her hands—open. Her eyes—shining, not with a joke, but with something profound and saline, as true as the ocean. The lie wasn't there.

"Do you believe me?"

I relaxed into the mattress and looked back at her, feeling a weight lift that I hadn't known was there. Feeling light enough that I just might sprout fairy wings and fly away. I smiled, breathed, looked her in the eye. "Yes," I said.

And I did. I really did.

Mermaids were real. Magic was real. Anything was possible. *Anything.* The fan hummed, the bed squeaked, and we otherwise sat in silence, but everything was different.

For a little while, until the noise returned, as it tends to when you are fifteen.

That was my last childhood summer as a camper, for I was soon to join the ranks of the working world. It was time to grow up, accept reality. The reality of a scientist, a naturalist, devotee of the wild and wondrous natural world that would need no fairytale creatures to woo me to awe.

Only then would I come to understand the real magic in Siobhan's gift. She had the uncanny ability to identify kids who suffered from too much reality and offer us not a fantasy world to escape to, but an alternate truth we were hungry for.

Because of her, I would keep an eye and ear out for the quiet truths, the alternate truths that might be lurking behind what we think we know. Just in case. Perhaps, one day, I'd have a magic tale of my own to share.

No mermaids, yet. But Siobhan, wherever you are, do I still believe you?

I do. I really do.

Baptisms

Dad blew bubbles and hummed into the tepid surface of the lake, pretending to be a boat. Flat on my belly, legs pumping, my arms encircled his neck. I squealed as he announced "submarine, going down," then ballooned my cheeks like a pufferfish. With my fingers clasped under his beard, he dove into the cool darkness. That was my favorite part.

I used to brag that I swam before I walked. In my first job teaching mother/infant swim classes I learned that's nothing special. You just need an adult to facilitate the process. Babies already know how to swim. Babies are not afraid of water. Unlike the four-year-olds who've learned fear of strangeness, who ask *what if* and whine *I can't*; babies take to water as if they were born from it. For they were. Their bodies remember.

~

The landscape of my youth was rich in waters. New England's geology collects ponds, lakes, and bogs like so many holy grails, pours them into brooks, streams, rivers, and eventually, the salty sea. Waters full of life— plant, animal, and in-between. Waters that join earth and sky. Not like the fluorescent-lit, sterile chlorine stink of pools.

I was an otter. I pinned my arms to my sides, locked my legs together, and arced my head forward, underwater. Kick and glide, weightless undulations. I blinked in the opaque haze, that liquid fog of northern lakes breached only by sunbeams illuminating the mucky bottom far below.

Underwater is the perfect combination of stimulation and sedation. You feel it on your body subtly, non-specifically, as temperature changes or arm hairs shifting in the currents. Hair undulates like kelp.

Underwater is the quiet room, the earplugs in, the mute button. Devoid of screaming kids, barking dogs, alarm bells, yelling parents, and slamming doors. Underwater is the dark cave, under the covers, midnight. No spotlights, no flashes, no glare. Underwater is solitary confinement, soft, scrumptious sensory deprivation. Under the water is death. Or, pre-birth. Same thing?

Sometimes I thought I belonged there.

I wanted to stay under but my lungs said *no*, so I rose, reluctantly.

A whistle shrieked. That tiny figure standing in brown sand under the weeping willow, that man waving a red float and yelling was the lifeguard.

"You're out too far; come in!"

"But I can swim!"

He didn't believe me, maybe because I was nine. I always made lifeguards nervous.

I crawl-stroked closer to shore where I could touch toes to

sand but I stayed in the water. I somersaulted, backflipped, and handstood. I floated on my back, arms and legs wobbling to keep my belly up and nose dry, my eyes closed against the sun. A spastic body doesn't have to behave in the water. It can twist and turn and flop and kick as hard as it wants, and still, the water will hold it.

I stayed in until my fingers were pruney, until my lips were blue, until Mom, Dad, Stepdad, or babysitter insisted I needed to eat or reapply sunscreen or go home because the sun was going down. Until then, I stayed in the water. "She's a fish!" they all said, and this made me happy.

~

We hesitated because we didn't bring our suits and we were fifteen years old. But it was still ninety degrees and muggy that August evening and the Rhode Island beach was deserted. We peeled off halter-tops and t-shirts, stepped out of jean-shorts and flip-flops, and ran whooping on scorching sand toward the waves. We kept running, taking giant steps over smaller breakers until it was deep enough to dive, and then we swam. Arm over arm, faces down we swam out and away, beyond our awkward adolescent bodies, out where we were strong and daring and independent. We splashed and laughed away our remaining nervousness as the sun sank behind the land. Until the earth said, *hush*. We stayed there, silent, bobbing like buoys. The cool water felt so good on naked skin. On sunburned backs, still-growing limbs, and on parts just waking up to the deliciousness of touch. After a while, as the stars blinked on, we spread arms and legs and floated on our backs, bare bodies in the twilight.

~

My sister and I tread water at the center of a radioactive green glacial lake in the middle of Glacier National Park. Our parents waved from shore. We waved back, our bodies glowing white in the chalky aquamarine. We looked around at the earth. Silver mountains rose and fell in a continuous circle, a 360-degree cardiogram. Below them, green triangles, a child's drawing of pine trees down to the huckleberry valleys embracing the round lake. We were at the midpoint of everything. Inside the earth and apart from it, looking out. We looked at each other, mirrored wide-eyed open-mouthed wonderment. Smiled, nodded. No words.

Our parents wouldn't understand. How could they ever understand Glacier National Park, from there?

~

I'd just stripped off fleece pants, long underwear, wool sweater, and thermal jacket and stood shivering in my bathing suit on a wooden dock on Hurricane Island, 75 miles northeast ("downeast") of Portland Maine. Pre-dawn wind gusted black diamonds on the water and white goosebumps on bare legs. It was early May in a place where even the Gulf Stream-warmed Atlantic dabbles in ice crystals.

But I was on an Outward Bound expedition and we all jumped in the ocean every day. No matter that winter had returned. No matter that the tide was out and the water was fifteen feet below the dock, white-capped and menacing. I was twenty-one, just graduated college, had no idea who to be, where to go, or what to do with my life stretching out before me like the Great Salt Desert and somehow I knew I needed this, so I jumped.

Flash forward. I stood naked in the snow by the Breitenbush river, in the mountains one hundred miles southeast of Portland Oregon, three thousand miles from where I was born. Snowflakes melted in my hair and eyelashes. The river was a deafening roar of white noise. I knew these rivers are snowmelt cold even in summer and it was New Year's Day. But I was thirty-one, just left my girlfriend, had no idea who to be, where to go, or what to do with the rest of my life stretching out before me like the Great Salt Desert and somehow I knew I needed this, so I jumped.

On contact my body spasmed, hands clawing to the surface and mouth gaping, gasping for air for inadequate lungs. Individual hair follicles on my head, neck, down my spine, and out to the tips of fingers and toes electrified. My skin ached, it stung, the current a swarm of bees finding my most tender parts. I flung my body to the edge, scaled the stairs or the slippery rocks, fought off death to get out, *get out!*

And I did. Back on dry earth, back in the air, my body radiated warmth. I took my time pulling on layers, stretching and grinning like the Cheshire cat just back from an invisible world.

We have to breathe air, need to live immersed in air but we are rarely aware of it. Earth is the playing field, the stage, the tabletop on which we spread our lives, but it's too dense to live inside of; we can't be there until after we die. The third element, fire, is no place for an animal body. We may seek its heat, whirl around the flames with kinetic fervor but deeper intimacy will always burn.

And water? We are more water than anything else. Our amphibious fetal bodies wore gill slits in salty wombs. Before hominids, before primates, before shrews, before reptiles, who were we? Fish.

Sometimes you need to go back to the beginning. Jump in, dive under. Swim, or just float. Remember where you came from. When you finally wriggle, claw, or crawl your way out onto dry earth you still may not know who to be, where to go or what to do, but you will find your legs strong beneath you, your lungs sipping air. At home.

~

Western Oregon is rich in waters. Rain or snow falls nine months of the year, frosting mountains, dripping off cedars, moss, and ferns, seeking rivers and creeks, and finally, the salty sea. Waters full of life—plant, animal, and in-between. Waters that joined earth and sky and made a new landscape home.

My favorite swimming hole was an eddy of the Sandy River where it paused on its journey from mountain to sea. I learned the Sandy in fall, yellow and red with cottonwood leaves and spawning Chinook; in winter thick and chocolate brown with rain, mud, and wayward trees; in spring harried and champagne-like with snowmelt; in summer languid green, dotted with fishermen and rafters, with dippers and mergansers.

One summer, up to my neck in languid green, I tip-toed on a rock, sculling arms behind me to keep from being carried downriver.

Something swam toward me.

Three somethings, moving upriver. Ducks? No. Beavers? No. I teetered and sculled. They came closer. One big thing and two little things, swimming directly for me.

The big thing stalled, two little things continued, closer, to fifteen feet away. Then, together, two furry round heads with white whiskers periscoped out of the water. Black jellybean eyes met mine. Black noses twitched above upturned kitten mouths. River otter kits.

They stared; I stared. They tilted their heads; I tilted my head. We sculled and floated, together. Then they turned back to Mom or Dad, and dove. I returned to the earth where I belonged. But I won't forget.

Before we walked, we swam.

Ablaze

"You have too much fire," my acupuncturist announced, reading the signs. My flushed face, burgundy tongue, rapid, jittery pulse. I pulled off my shirt and lay face down on the soft cotton sheets of the treatment table. Lightning quick, she flicked tiny needles into my skin. Pinpricks of electricity zinged the top of my head, back of my neck, along both sides of my spine. Then the webbing between thumb and forefinger, and the space between ankle and Achilles. She lay a cool hand on the small of my back and breathed, "Rest. I'll be back later." I exhaled deeply, savoring this pleasure on the knife-edge of pain.

When I was small my father taught me to extinguish candles with bare fingers. I learned young to reach for flame.

A childhood of summers spent at sleep-away camps sparked an affection for the dry snap crackle of campfires. Eastern white pine, red oak, and paper birch. Charred marshmallows and crispy black hotdogs. Sitting cross-legged on pine needles I leaned toward the flames, staring, as if determining whether friend or foe. The bold scarlets and ochres drew me in; the elusive cobalts and violets kept me there. Unable to look away, though my eyes burned.

There were other fires of childhood, stoked by a father who hit a mother. By a mother who wailed. By nights spent wide awake willing myself not to listen to the shouting. Acid burned in the pit of my stomach. When I was five I shattered the glass of the front door with my fist. I wanted out.

Eighteen years later, when I did get out, fire stayed with me. I moved west, found the incense smoke of juniper, fir, and cedar. Wild singing fires, ardent laughing fires, and fervent naked dancing fires. Outdoor school naturalist fires I arranged with my own hands, then lit and supervised like unruly children. And the cleansing fires of prescribed burns.

Adulthood ignited other flames. Sensual heat of skin on skin. Men. Women. Both. Spring fevers, summer passions, fall restlessness, and winter smolderings.

I learned to create fire without matches. That with the right fuel and fortitude, friction transforms wood into smoking black dust, a dust that when added to tinder, I could blow into flame. The combustion of my own breath.

With creation came destruction. To embrace fire is to invite both.

Mysterious hives, inflamed joints, explosive anger, mania. A searing rage I tried to cut out of me with razors and shards of glass. The same burn that drove me into tattoo studios to endure hours of needles drilling colors into skin. Inky flames forever on my back.

I watched a father drown in whiskey. Saw the spark go out in his eyes. His heart. His body. Until he was extinguished. Not everyone can take the heat. But I learned young to reach for flame.

I fanned my own fire. I stalked it, moved wherever it led me. Zig-zagging across the country, I zip-lined off bridges in New Hampshire, banded raptors in Nevada, tended bobcats in Florida, massaged at a hot springs commune in Oregon, taught fire ecology in the Colorado Rockies, and learned wilderness survival in Washington. Fire isn't linear. The right combination of fuel, air, and spark will burn where it can.

One winter I sought out the cleansing fire of a New Year's ceremony, a community bonfire fed with offerings and prayers. The leader raked the day-long fire into glowing coals as twilight advanced. That frozen day, too clear and cold to snow, I removed boots and wool socks, rolled up pants, scrunched up long underwear, and stepped toward the glow. Then walked calmly, almost floating, onto the coals. I felt only a tingling ache in my toes and the elation of a phoenix resurrected from her own ashes. My feet turned black but did not burn. The key is to keep moving.

She came to take the needles out. Flicked them out of my feet, hands, back, neck, and head. I sat up and pulled on my shirt, breathing evenly. Calm for the moment. She told me to go easy on spicy food, beating sun, scalding baths. To avoid stressful situations. I savored the ache on the knife-edge of ecstasy, and said nothing.

Speed

I was part vampire. My friends and I decided on this one sleepover night after catching a clip of the late-night horror movie and deciding my teeth were far too pointy for human teeth. I found this a better explanation than the dentist's declaration that I'd been grinding them every night since the age of five. In fourth grade, when the eye doctor said my eyes let in too much light and that I should always wear dark glasses, that sealed the deal. In bright sunlight when I didn't, and sometimes even when I did, I got terrible headaches. Still do.

My skin is equally touchy. As a lifeguard and swim teacher in my teen years, I was the only one slathering on SPF 15, the highest in those days, while my coworkers shimmered in baby oil. Still, they bronzed while I moved along my skin tone's spectrum between alabaster and lobster. Beyond lobster, I blister: penny-sized skin bubbles which peel to reveal fetal pink beneath. If I spend long hours in full sun several days in a row, whether or not I've been faithful with today's SPF 100 that can keep me toward the pale end of my spectrum, my skin will rash anyway. Intensely itchy sun allergy bumps varnish my chest and neck. Painful sores erupt in my mouth and on my lips. A few years ago, when my doctor learned that I worked and spent much of my free time outside, he began a sentence with WHEN *you get skin cancer*.

I currently live in the Pacific Northwest on the west (wet) side of the Cascades Mountains. I spent ten years in Portland with thirty-six inches of rainfall over 222 cloudy days per year and then moved three hours north to one more inch and four more overcast days per year, the cloudiest region of the continental U.S., the perfect setting for the most famous vampire movies in history where all that mist and ferns and moss and pendulous lichens did not need to be staged; it actually looks like that here.

And yet, I have to shake my head at my childhood self and remind her of two important flaws in the vampire theory (now more knowledgeable on such matters having taken a college course on "Vampire Myth and Legend" under the guise of Slavic folklore. Liberal Arts.) First, though my iron count is often low, I have never thirsted for blood. A rare juicy steak where my jagged teeth come in handy, sure, but not plain blood. Second, the thing I do thirst for is exactly what vampires tend to avoid. Sunshine.

I am ravenous for it, can't get enough of it, am physically pained when I know it's shining out there and I can't be outside in it. If sunshine were a drug, it would be speed.

Technically? Light *is* speed. Electromagnetic waves or photon particles—both are true and neither is quite right—no matter how deeply we dive, how closely we look, all we know for sure is that the basic element of light is motion. That brighter light means more motion, faster vibrations. This isn't movement we can see with our eyes but at some level, probably multiple levels, we feel it. And I'm hooked. I lust for it, want to soak in it, absorb it, become it, then more.

~

"Slow down, Heather; you're so erratic." My ballet teacher to me, at fifteen. I couldn't help but move as fast as the energy around me, pulled in multiple directions, undulating and spinning like a top. Stereo speakers throbbed the orchestral version of heavy metal: piccolos shrieked, trumpets blared, tympanis thumped, and cymbals crashed while twelve other tutu-ed teenagers twirled nearby; how could I possibly slow down? Once you start spinning, how do you stop? If, as Newton's first law of motion states, a body in motion will stay in motion unless acted on by an external force, what if that external force is more motion, more speed?

What started that motion in the first place? What animated the musicians, electrified the stereo, charged the pulsing hormonal teenagers? The source of us all, sunlight. We like to say our bodies are mostly water. But without sunlight, we'd just be puddles.

Plants get to drink sunlight. Their physical bodies transform sunshine into the sugars they need to grow. More sunlight, more potential growth. To maximize growth, they lean, bend, and reach for the sun as if they too can't get enough. Speed up their movements with time-lapse photography, and you will see a perfectly choreographed ballet of swirling, undulant greenery, each individual body magnetized to the sun's direction by day, by season, and amidst their changing landscapes.

Inside I'd been pacing and watching the sky and the forecast because it was supposed to rain that week and what if that was my last dose for a while? So I gave in and went outside to sweat on my towel on the shaggy grass and feel useless and a little guilty, getting nothing done that I needed to and much done that I didn't like burning my chest and nose again.

Because I also needed my fix. Needed to soak it up for the next day when I would have to work inside. Needed to soak it up for fall and winter and spring when it might be raining even though it never seems to rain as consistently as it used to and seems to get sunnier and hotter every year. I needed to soak it up until a supposedly inevitable skin cancer forces me to quit, but in the meantime, I would spend yet another summer day half-naked, flipping from front to back, back to front, reapplying sunscreen. You could tell the time by my shadow as I sundialed my way around the yard to maximize the rays on my skin. A book, my journal, and binoculars forgotten by my side, the illusion of productivity.

On the surface, I was dazed, sedated, slow as a sloth. Eyes closed, dozing in and out of catnaps, muscles twitching. Inside I was dancing, leaping, and spinning, positively euphoric. Giddy as a boozed-up college kid. Content as a doped-up junkie. If I were a cat, I'd have been purring.

Snakes sunbathe. Lizards too. Turtles clamber over each other for the best spot on the log sticking out of the beaver pond. Alligators crawl out of cypress swamps to bask on the mowed strips by paths and roadways. Though they can't drink the sun directly, reptiles utilize external fire to maintain internal fire. If the sun's light and heat can do some of the work of food, why waste energy finding food when lying still can fuel you the same? Recent studies show that some reptiles use sunlight to deliberately regulate healthy levels of vitamin D. Lizards who aren't getting enough in their diet will spend more time sunning. Somehow their bodies know, and they seek out what they need.

Frogs and salamanders are ectothermic too, but their moist permeable skin can't take much direct sunlight. They need to use it indirectly by choosing warm locations. Finding food more often. Accepting life at a slower pace. Though they might enjoy a good basking and the energy boost it would give them, they would be in danger of ending up like the desiccated earthworm on the driveway after the rain. Have you ever seen a salamander run? Dart and skitter up walls or along fences, zoom over lichen-blackened rocks? Me neither. The most you might hope for from a salamander, even on the hottest summer day, is a determined waddle.

We mammals carry sunshine within us; the furnace is always lit. So why risk burns, blisters, skin cancers, DNA damage, and the likelihood of resembling a geriatric crocodile? Vitamin D is the usual answer, and a good one. As for what that one measly vitamin does for us: "at least 1,000 different genes governing virtually every tissue in the body are now thought to be regulated by 1,25-dihydroxyvitamin D_3, the active form of the vitamin, including several involved in calcium metabolism and neuromuscular and immune system functioning."[7] It does a lot. Lack of vitamin D and UV radiation as a whole has been linked to decreased bone density and cancers, including Hodgkin's lymphoma, breast, ovarian, colon, pancreatic, and prostate cancers. Growing evidence also suggests that vitamin D deficiency can contribute to higher incidences of multiple sclerosis, diabetes, and hypertension.

Fine. But why not just take vitamin D supplements? Because as important as that one little vitamin might be, there is so much more to our bodies' thirst for sunlight than just nutritional value. Despite what the nutrition industry might suggest, you just can't get sunshine in a pill with your morning orange juice.

Bright sunlight increases serotonin production, which makes us happy, then in darkness transforms into melatonin, which helps us sleep. This isn't a process triggered inside our bodies; our skin makes these chemicals directly from sunlight. Human skin also has receptors to turn sunlight into endorphins, natural opiates, and to manufacture dopamine, natural speed. Our eyes in particular drink in the light and pump out the dopamine. More sunlight, more happy chemicals.

Plants make food; we make drugs. Are we biologically smart enough to seek out what we need, to regulate ourselves like lizards, protect ourselves like frogs?

∼

On the outside I appeared a typical, well-adjusted suburban teenager. On the inside, the equally typical swirling mess of confusion and desire. I'd quit ballet to spend more time with a boyfriend. Then a different boyfriend. Out of my leotard and into ripped jeans and a black Depeche Mode t-shirt, I still spun like a top. It's just that the soundtrack had changed to something more like Violent Femmes' *Blister In The Sun*.

Truth or Dare? Dare, always. Strip games in the basement. Spin the bottle in the treehouse with four boys and only one other girl and a full bottle of cinnamon schnapps; hair-sprayed metalhead Ratt's hand up my shirt. Sitting on the kitchen floor, drinking just a little from all the bottles in Stepdad's liquor cabinet. Midnight showings of *Rocky Horror Picture Show*— Let's do the Time Warp Again. Arms around Ed's waist, zooming through the woods on his moped. Jägermeister shots at a beach bonfire, magic mushroom tea before river rafting, vodka punch with Crystal Light in the graveyard. Sneaking Mike out of boarding school after vodka and raspberry ginger ale in the hip teacher's apartment then wrestling in the back stairway of the library while oblivious prep school boys studied on the other side of the wall and then inevitably, sex. Hands in each others' hair, grasping and clawing as if one of us was in danger of falling off a cliff at any moment. Sex in the woods behind his dorm. Sex in his VW bug. On the pool table. Under the pool table. On the phone. In the basement with his hand over my mouth because his parents were upstairs. At the town playground after dark, Led Zeppelin on the tapedeck. Always with the animal intensity of the first time, or maybe the last time. Scratch marks on our backs. Patchouli oil on our flannel shirts, matching anarchy symbols Sharpied on our Converse All-Stars.

Piercing my ears again, watching the blood run. Dragging my knuckles across the brick walls of my high school, watching my fist turn blue. Slicing razor blades across ankles, chest, wrists, watching the blood run. Not to die, but to live.

Dancing, if you could call it dancing, in basements, then nightclubs, always in darkness, music deafening, thumping, grinding. Bouncing, jumping, spinning.

Was I hungry for something I lacked or trying to burn up excess?

"Speed is a response to both danger and desire," –Terry Tempest Williams.[8] Danger *and* desire. What's the difference between running toward or fleeing from? If light is paradoxically both particles and waves, maybe direction is similarly slippery. Forward, backward, it all depends which way you're facing. Zoom out and there is only spinning.

Amphetamine. Benzedrine. Dexedrine. Adderall. Crystal Meth. Speed. Chemicals of downward spiraling sore-covered toothless desperation in dank alleys and backwoods shacks. Prescriptions for obesity, narcolepsy, and ADHD in sterile doctor's offices. A little dopamine fix or a big one; what's your pleasure? Alertness, sexual arousal, euphoria? Improved cognitive function and nerve growth? Anxiety, paranoia, mood swings, psychosis? Heart attack, convulsions, coma, stroke?

Danger or desire, junkie or vampire. Big-brained ape or lizard or frog or spiraling green sapling. What if all cravings stem from the same primal longing for sunlight?

~

The fourth of July dawned sunny *and* hot. Not Pacific Northwest coastal summer warm but New Orleans sweltering hot. Here, we don't know what to do with that. You can see it in how we peer at each other from half-closed lids like cats with twitchy tails who might pounce at any second. Driving is dangerous, feet heavy on gas pedals, grown boys flaunting their plumage, their fitness, their mating prowess. Like the muscle-shirt man in the convertible who tailgated me, then revved to pass when I pulled over. Both of us considered flipping the other the bird, but people get shot in weather like that.

Everyone was *in* heat, the volume of life cranked up to a static whine, everything whizzing and whirring in high-definition, like the 3D Imax with stereo surround-sound and motion simulation, and I just can't ride that ride anymore. Moth, back away from the flame. We know how that turns out.

I stayed home, sought the source. On my beach towel in my quiet yard with a book, my binoculars, and a gin and tonic for good measure, I didn't have to watch families fight, teenagers play chicken and run off the road, children scream, or dogs croon. I didn't have to smell cigarettes or kerosene or hot tar on creosote. I could hear fireworks, or maybe that was the neighbors shooting their guns, but far off through the woods I didn't have to watch them goad each other and wave their guns around drunk and stupid, my heart in my throat waiting for one to go off at the wrong time pointed in the wrong direction.

I lay there in my dark glasses, restless and twitching but safe from danger and desire. Still, my head throbbed and my lips burned.

A bit of thunder—a mountain lion's purr—and the rain came.

It plucked the shingles like guitar strings, windchimed onto the stones below my open windows. Lullabyed onto the bigleaf maples, cottonwoods, cedars, and me. Cooling mist wafted in on the sweet breeze, as if I was on the precipice of a great waterfall. Right then, I was.

A robin perched on the elderberry at the forest edge fluffed up and shook out like a puppy after a swim. Deeper in the woods, a Swainson's thrush began to sing. Like rain falling up, she spiraled her flutey harmonies and punctuated it with a drip call note.

My head cleared. My lungs opened. I exhaled as if I'd been holding my breath. How long had I been holding my breath? I felt back in my body, safely contained, home again as if after an arduous journey.

Back inside, I boiled water for tea and watched the steam swirl up from the Earl Grey into the cooling air, watched it dancing and swaying with the mist. I myself was still. Inside and out. No euphoria, but also no dark glasses, no twitching, and no burning. I sat for hours, blanket on my lap, watching. Steam swirled, mist rose, rain dripped on the trees, the ferns, the moss. And I, released from spinning. For the meantime.

Undertow

The noise hit me first. I flinched as water clapped sand and the clatter ricocheted off chipped white-painted concrete breakwaters, condominium tower walls, and the metal bars of the fifth-floor balcony where I stood. This was not the gentle white noise static of the northern oceans I knew, the expansive joyful roar of water tumbling into the waiting arms of a broad continental shore. This was the sound of heavy artillery. Each wave a shotgun blast, ringing in my ears. This was violence.

"What?" I yelled over the cacophony. My mother was saying something.

"Welcome to paradise!"

I smiled for them. She and her husband Lauriston—Lorry for short—had come to this same rental in the northwest corner of Puerto Rico for five years, first for a week visiting friends, then up to a month on their own after retirement. Humble beach apartments stacked into a highrise with boxy balconies facing tropical sunset. What's not to love? It was February for goodness sake. Maybe I didn't fly away from the slushy snow and icy roads of New England winter as they did, but February in the Pacific Northwest is still raw and cool with rain. Drippy, drizzly, ebullient green mossy, hunker down with tea and a blanket winter. I now wore a tank top and shorts, hot sun on naked skin, and squinted at a sapphire sky and marbled blue ocean. Blue that went on forever, no end in sight, with an equally incessant soundtrack. I should have been ecstatic.

Four-sided cells of thick concrete protected the privacy of neighbors and framed the ocean beyond, as on a top-heavy oceanliner. I walked to the edge to grip the white-painted steel bars and looked down. A patio of faded stones held scattered wicker lounge chairs, three umbrellaed tables, and a small electric blue inground pool. Seven-foot metal bars caged the patio. Immediately beyond and only slightly below churned the frothy Atlantic.

"What?" My mother was speaking again.

"There used to be beach here, but every year there was less and now we just have the patio. But we can walk down to where there's still sand. We'll..."

Another crack obliterated her final words. I smiled, nodded, felt the sun already burning my arms, and watched another breaker crash below the bars and whip up clouds of brown sand in the surf. The brash aftershocks echoed down the beach, up to the walls, into my brain.

I was probably just tired. Four red-eye flights through five airports, a complete change of scenery, climate, and season, with a four-hour time-change to boot. That would make anyone feel like a zombie in the twilight zone. I had the next six days there with my mother and her husband, their graduation-from-graduate-school gift to me, to settle in to a place and experience I could never think to afford for myself. I got to visit the paradise of the postcards; taste the winter of the snowbirds.

It didn't yet seem any more real in person. Just louder.

The next morning I woke before sunrise from crackling crashing dreams, the wave noise still prominent, but the wind had calmed. The sea was less churning—more like the thunder of a summer lightning storm, less like the eye of a hurricane.

My eyes were hungry for the earth and since the bedroom window was too high to see out, I moved to the kitchen and cranked open the dark slats. To the south along the beach—a Tetris puzzle of flat rooftops huddled together with little space in between. Terracotta shingled cupolas decorated the skyscape, and glossy black Caribbean martins darted and dove around them after a morning insect hatch.

I craned my neck to look east, away from the water and toward the sunrisen glow of the coastal town of Stella. Beyond that, a swath of green painted a hillside with the unmistakable cartoon look of palm trees poking up here and there, but also leafy green trees with branching trunks more like I was used to. I exhaled and unclenched a part of my stomach I hadn't realized was clenched. I was still on earth.

I made coffee and sat with my cup in one of the white plastic balcony chairs, feet up on the bars to watch the morning show. Brown pelicans hovered, then dove, spinning and corkscrewing aerodynamic bullets into the sea, popping up again to rest on the surface and, if they were lucky, gulping down breakfast. The fishing must have been good then because at least a dozen of them alternately twirled, dove, and buoyed.

Human fishermen sought the ocean's bounty too. One steered a small motorboat while his partner perched at the bow looking down, arms full of net. I could sense the weight of the mass of nylon as he bent his knees a little and twisted to heft it into the water. Peered down, paused, and hauled it back in for another go.

Crack, a wave hit, followed by the ripping sound as it raced down the beach. Then another. I couldn't see them break but I could see the energy rolling in, liquid mountains that rose and fell every few seconds. Worlds collided and combusted. I watched and listened. Let the ocean hypnotize me. I was fully rested but still felt oddly drugged.

"Morning!" I jumped as my mother put her hand on my shoulder. I hadn't heard her come up behind me. "You want to go swimming? We should go soon before the wind picks up. This is as calm as it gets."

I turned to see they were already in bathing suits and hopped up to join them.

We stepped through the metal gate a short while later and walked down the partially sand-buried steps to stand against the seawall watching the crashers advance toward us. They were taller up close, and just as loud. They broke at our feet. Nobody else was in the ocean here, or anywhere near here, that I could see. Another retired couple sat up on the deck by the pool, sheltered by umbrella, sunhats, and sunglasses. "You're brave!" they yelled, and I felt proud of Mom and her jovial, still somewhat new-to-me husband after my stepfather. If they can do this, surely I can?

"Just watch for a bit," Lorry shouted, "and wait for a smaller one. Then swim like crazy." We saw our moment and seized it, running, hopping, and then diving under the churning.

We did it! Escaped the breakers to mingle with the blue mountains. The water was comfortably cool, almost but not quite warm. Mom and Lor smiled and bobbed with their Styrofoam noodles, and I reclined to float on my back. I'm a decent swimmer but an excellent floater. Some bodies are buoys.

Out there you could feel the intensity. I spread my arms and legs and tilted my head up a little in an attempt to keep water from sloshing into my eyes and nose. Up and down. Up and down, like seafoam. A pelican dove nearby, and I watched as it bounced up from the deep to rest on the surface at eye level.

A darker, thinner shadow passed in front of the sun, and I looked up to see long tapered wings and a long forked tail. The telltale shape of the tropical seabird with a marvelous name. Magnificent frigatebird! I spoke the name to the waves, tasted the delicious syllables in my mouth, savored them for later.

I'm not sure what makes frigatebirds so magnificent, except maybe that they spend much of their lives flying over oceans and rarely land. To feed, they skim food from the water's surface or pirate it from other birds. Otherwise, they ride the thermals like kites.

Down on the surface, I didn't feel at all that magnificent. More like a forgotten sea creature, bleached and flailing. Or maybe, remembered, and hated. The ocean's prodigal children. The wind picked up and a smaller crest slapped me in the face, leaving me sputtering.

I was exhausted. Even floating was so much work out there, riding the rollers, jostling in the washing machine. I realized I was panting, close to hyperventilating. I looked over at my mother and she pointed at the shore. I nodded, relieved.

The ocean didn't release us easily. We had to fight for it, swim hard with the ingoing waves even as the undertow pulled us backward. Forward and back, up and down, and finally, jubilantly, I was tossed out on the sand. I crawled the final few feet. Bad form for a former swim teacher and lifeguard, but I was past caring. This didn't remotely resemble the chlorine pools or languid lakes of my youth. This beast was fierce.

I wobbled to my feet and gripped the steel railing to brace against a wave that had snuck up behind me, then walked up the stairs to the deck. After rinsing salt and sand under a freshwater spigot, I spread my towel and collapsed onto a lounge chair to dry out.

After a couple minutes of exhilaration, I faded back into the heat and ocean breeze, completely worn out. I slathered a new layer of sunscreen over still-sandy skin, and flopped back down. I dozed off and dreamt a David Lynch movie of indecipherable symbols, people becoming animals, fighting like hyenas, speaking in tongues. Something huge and amorphous stalked me.

A wave's report jolted me upright, and from a nearby chair, Lor asked if I was ready to join them for a walk on the beach. We headed out the back of the highrise and down the street. Past a jungle-lush fenced compound with peacocks and fancy chickens, past adobe chateaus with blooming azaleas and bouganvilla, past humble block houses with low rider cars and radios blaring.

The neighborhood beach access was at the end of a dirt road where lay the ruins of a chateau, walls disconnected and at odd angles, melting into the sea. It was hard to know how long the wreck had been here or how long it would stay. The ocean would take it back in her own time.

We stepped over smaller chunks of concrete and exposed rebar and through a small colony of snakeplant, that ubiquitous low-maintenance potted plant of fluorescent-lit offices up north. Though *Sansevieria trifasciata* hails from tropical West Africa, it seemed to thrive there in nutrient-poor sand and salt air.

We found the beach, real sand, and we kicked off flip-flops and moved seaward to the strip where it stayed wet and wouldn't burn our feet. The sand was dark, black in patches but mostly dark gray, sometimes pebbly. In places there were only rocks, and though mostly rounded, we hobbled and limped over them with tender feet. The ocean still had work to do there, in that place of gentler waves.

We walked past crooked shacks and looming hotels. Past feral fields where locals drove right up to the edge on grassy sand. We hopped over or ducked under fishing line and leaning palm trees. Nodded and smiled at those we passed but mostly kept our heads down, searching for the unburied treasure I'd been told I would find there. Sea glass.

Once sharp shards of ordinary discarded bottles or occasionally, kitchen glassware, window or auto glass, tumbled, ground smooth, and frosted by the sea. It takes at least twenty years, my mother told me, and up to fifty for genuine sea glass. I remember finding a piece every now and then on the Rhode Island beaches of my childhood, how it was strangely more exciting than the discarded shells of sea creatures. Maybe it was the rarity, or perhaps, the simple beauty of jewel-like colors in the sunlight. I thought they were gifts from the ocean, especially for me.

On the west coast of Puerto Rico, despite crowded beaches and throngs of tourists, sea glass abounds. So much glass can be found there, they say, from a combination of annual rains and other erosive forces uncovering historic island landfills, from beach parties and a relatively lax stewardship ethic, and, it being a small island in a chain of islands, flotsam from shipwrecks. Multiple sea trade routes ran through the Caribbean, moving molasses and rum. Some ships wrecked in the waves. Others were plundered by pirates.

Mom had her net bag ready, and Lorry and I wore shorts with deep pockets. I'd seen the collection they had at the apartment, which they said they were happy to share, but I was eager to find some of my own. Each day, each tide, even each wave can scour the beach anew. Among the pebbles and sand, glass gets sucked out, tumbled and tossed, buried or uncovered. Coincident with commercial glass use, greens and browns are common. Blues and reds are rare.

The rocky, pebbled areas are best, the places where the waves windchime as water moves through stone. The places where the ocean tosses rock against ankles. I realized why my mother had bruises on her ankles and shins. Soon I would too. There is a cost, but I was willing to pay.

We walked and stooped and grabbed at colors, held them up to the light, weighed whether they were worth saving. We stumbled and limped and lunged. My pockets grew heavy and sagged. We stopped speaking to each other, didn't even look up to say hi to those we passed. Most of them were doing the same. Heads down, on the hunt for shiny things. We were diminished to sounds, grunts and squeals, and holding up our prizes before pocketing them and returning to the search. Or, when they didn't measure up, too sharp and new, or too plain, we tossed them back. How quickly I joined their obsession. How easily I regressed.

When I got too hot, I waded farther into the ocean, let the salty, sandy waves batter me for a time. Then returned to the hunt. Mom held up a piece of blue, and Lor and I *ooh*ed and *ah*ed appreciatively. She was the best at this.

What odd animals we are. We make glass by melting together what is basically beach sand—silicon dioxide, quartz—with other trace elements for resiliency and color. Glass is the process of putting rocks back together. We use our homemade rock tools and vessels then we toss them back to the earth, and the place older than that, the sea. The sea does her work to break them down again and there we were, grasping at shards of trash in the process of unbecoming. They were not gifts of the ocean. Nor were we pirates plundering treasure. More like crows or vultures, feasting at the dump.

When we were sufficiently tired, hungry, and burning, we returned the way we came along the beach to the snakeplant and the ruins and then through the town to the highrise. We did our best to pre-rinse our outer layers of sand, salt, sweat, and sunscreen at the deck spigot before heading up to take turns with real showers.

In clean shorts and a tanktop, lotioned and lighter, I gathered up the start of my sea glass collection. Two greens, one brown, a white, and a tiny shred of blue. The ones worth saving. They were soft, cool and smooth to the touch, and rounded, no edges. No longer translucent, but cloudy, opaque. Infused with salt and sand.

Mom leaned over the counter examining her latest treasures, determining whether they would be added to the plate full of glass she planned to bring home, or the plateful she planned to leave in the rental or maybe throw back to the waves. Lor was already in the easy chair with his book and a snack.

I got some leftover potato salad from the fridge, took my book out to the balcony, and tucked a chair back against the shaded corner under the painting of an anchor so I wouldn't have to reapply sunscreen. As a wave's explosion reentered my awareness I realized that I could still feel the ocean. Looking out at the roiling blue I was no longer on a stationary ship; I was moving too. Maybe it was my time spent in the water that morning, the kinesis still acting on me. Or maybe it was just the whole seascape working on me. Taking me in.

A house sparrow appeared through the bars near my feet. *Cheep!*

Hi sparrow, I said, and he *cheeped* again then disappeared. I held my book in my lap and stared out. I tried to read a few pages, but the waves brought me back here, now.

Now.

Now! It was always now, and now was stretching. I moved from the balcony to the living room, lay flat on the couch. Mom made piña coladas, as you do in the fantasy. We cranked closed the shutters against the afternoon sun. We didn't speak much, because the wind picked up and waves got louder in the afternoon. Eventually we turned on the shell encrusted table lamps. Sunset was subtle that night, too many afternoon clouds. We retired soon after. We hadn't done much of anything, but we were worn out.

I lay in the cool white sheets under the whirring fan and listened to the waves and the night sounds between them—first a few crickets, then a strange new sound I would later learn was the local tree frog. Coqui. A cousin of my Pacific chorus frog which *creee-eeeeks* in the night, this frog sang a staccato CO-KEE! CO-KEE!

Waves. Frogs. Waves.

I was marooned there in that odd Neverland for five more days. Nothing to do but give in to it. Let it have its way with me.

I swam. I walked. I dove after pirate scraps, collecting bruises. I napped in the sun, then the shade. I read. Started drinking earlier every day. When Mom wasn't mixing, I made rum and cokes with lime. Lots of ice. Sit. Lie down. Close the shades. Listen to the ocean. Listen.

Sun and surf and salt and rum; good lord would I come out the other side? How does anyone?

One morning we went out for brunch with Mom and Lorry's friends, inland. Green grass and trees and songbirds and no… noise. I ate eggs benedict and drank Cuban coffee with raw sugar and we had normal conversations with each other and the waitress who'd moved back there from New York and everything felt normal again.

But back to the edge of the world, the edge of reality, I was in painless purgatory. I had become one of the pale and reddening zombies moving between sun and shade, shade and sun, pool and lounge chair. This was the ocean's pace. Loud and slow. I could watch the pelicans dive, the frigatebirds circle, and the horizon stretch away to nothing in three directions. Watch the ocean devour the sand, the seawalls, the buildings, and me.

Another couple of Mom and Lorry's friends arrived from Connecticut; they would take the second bedroom for a week to overlap before my family headed north and left the place to them. Because I was the freeloader, I moved to sleep on the balcony. I threw a sheet over the easy chair cushions and tucked them against one of the balcony walls. I spent my final two nights sleeping there in the wind and noise. I retired early, left the older adults to their catching up in the lighted inside, and I, though over forty, was once again the small child on the trundle bed listening to the grownups. Sometimes time moves backward.

Night was the loudest, sonic booms and ricocheting echoes. I was mesmerized. Every wave shouted *Wake Up*. Every lull in between a held breath. Everything, becoming. Everything poised, and the spaces were eternities. I began to like that space, that frozen kinesis. Even if I was forgetting things. Even if I forgot who I was.

Crash-remember-*crash*-forget-*crash*-who?-*crash*-what?

There was no who, not even a what. The ocean is older than all that.

I surrendered. The waves. The noise. The wind, howling, but warm, thick and tepid like your insides.

I discovered—the usual noise in my head? It was gone.

For the first time I could remember, inside, I was quiet. My inner voice was still there, but no longer seemed to have anything to say. Like the early days of television when the broadcasts ended for the day and all twelve channels turned to static fuzz. Like time moving backward. Back to the beginning.

On my second to last day we took a drive to another beach to see a historic lighthouse and watch the surfers. Canopies spanned the parking lot where vendors sold their wares to locals and tourists alike—bottles of water and orange soda, cheap trinkets and expensive jewelry. Heat rose from the blacktop and hung in the air around us. It was an intense heat I hadn't otherwise felt there, and I realized the ocean and her winds had kept this from us. In an overheated daze we picked things up, put them down again, moved on. We moved slowly, heavily, like tortoises. Sweat trickled into my eyes, stinging with the latest layer of SPF 50 that didn't seem to be working anymore because my skin was burning and rashing anyway.

A colorful flash alerted me to a new bird, striking orange and black like an oriole but with a longer beak. It seemed to be making a home in an abandoned woodpecker hole. I walked up to a table of jewelry and asked the vendors if they knew what kind of bird that is. A grandmother peered out from under the canopy and smiled *Oh, yes, that bird is special. That is our Puerto Rican Troupial.*

She switched back to Spanish to speak with some locals then English to tell my mother about a piece of sea glass jewelry. Colorful glass pieces were threaded onto nylon cord or wrapped with silver or copper wire, making necklaces, bracelets, earrings, keychains, even windchimes. All, we learned, from sea glass found on the island. The woman and her adult daughter had run the little shop for years.

I found an anklet of braided black nylon with a single piece of soft blue glass and asked the woman about it. Most blues are from medicine bottles, poison bottles, or inkwells, she told us. *You can know this?* We were thrilled, and like children began to point and ask about the different colors and textures. She seemed happy to share her expertise, this naturalist of sea glass. She pulled out a large catalog and pointed to the most common glasses found on the island, told us when they were made and how they were used. The most common greens, browns, and whites—soda, beer, and wine bottles. A few drinking glasses, milk bottles. The rarer jade, amber, or dark olive— those are whiskey, rum, or antique wine bottles. She told us that if we brought her a piece, she could make jewelry for us.

Our next day's walk, my final morning before I headed north again, I had a new purpose. Find sea glass worthy of jewelry. I had a couple potentials in my collection, but I wanted something special.

I wasn't sure of it at first; it was definitely a keeper but not necessarily unique. Not blue or red, anyway. It looked almost black, dark green with a hint of midnight, like the ocean. But when I held it up to the light I saw an odd turquoise glow. The smooth triangle felt good in my hand. It felt like the one. It was mine.

We returned to the vendor on the way to the airport. The grandmother told me I had a good eye. My piece was an antique, a shard of a wine bottle from the '30s, she thought. Mateus wine—a Portuguese rosé that used to be bottled in teal and dark blue-green flasks. She spun a silver spiral onto it and put it on a silver chain. The weight of it felt good around my neck.

I heard a cheerful whistle and looked over to see the Troupial disappear into its cavity. I would learn later that they are considered "nest pirates;" that bird had usurped some other bird's nest and claimed it for its own. An easy label, to be sure, a way to turn up our noses at animals who take what once belonged to others. Like us.

We move in, we claim, we take. We build up and then throw away, thinking only of moving forward, getting ahead. Progress! We colonialists, we capitalists, we consumers, we are riding the biggest wave of all. Whether we fight it or do not, this wave will crash. We know this. But what is harder to think of is what comes after. Ocean time consists of equal parts forward and back. Back to dissolution, to obliteration, back to the beginning. When the ocean takes us back, it won't be gentle, nor quiet. It will be violent. Deafening.

I hadn't been on that desert island long enough to be transformed, to be pummeled smooth as glass. Soon I would take three planes home to soft misty rain and quiet green forest, to my job and my rented apartment with my things and the voice in my head telling me everything is alright, and my world would go back to normal. But when I felt the weight of my pirate necklace hanging from my neck, I would remember the noise, the discomforting thunderous voice of the ocean, shouting, *Wake Up*.

My parents would return to Puerto Rico that next winter, and then no more. September of the following year, Hurricane Maria's storm surge would obliterate the deck, scoop out the concrete foundation, and topple the highrise like a child's sandcastle.

Dismembering

The knife in my right hand carved through the limb of bitter cherry and sliced easily into the tip of my left thumb, denser than air but more porous than wood. When I pulled it out of me, the blade was clean.

I raised my thumb to see a bead of crimson meet the November air. It swelled and bulged, threatening to spill over onto the earth. Just as surface tension succumbed to gravity I pressed thumb to wood. My blood entered the bitter cherry, which dead and sapless, drank it in all the quicker. I held it there and resumed carving. The limb was becoming a spoon.

Rain plinked and plunked and gurgled and rushed all around as if we were in an air bubble at the bottom of a river, our bubble a tarp shelter and our river a rainforest. Cedars bobbed and shimmied like octopi and cottonwoods swayed like prehistoric grasses. Waterfalls formed where the plastic was secured to live branches, until wind gusts burst them into fine mists.

My hair and the back of my wool sweater glistened with moisture, but the front of me was warm and dry. At the center of our circle of fir benches and cottonwood rounds, a fire devoured cedar and fir logs and exhaled heat.

A human animal squatted nearby, hands open to the glow. Another speared a piece of deer flesh onto a green alder stick and held it just above the flames. The rest of us sat around the circle, carving, sanding, weaving.

I didn't know most of them, not in the way we normally speak of knowing. I didn't know their histories, their families, their jobs, or aspirations. I barely knew their names. But I saw the firelight dance in their eyes as it must have in mine and I recognized different shades of my experience in them. The pained squint of a young man intent on perfection. The surprised satisfaction of an elder man fingering his first roughening callouses. The peaceful, relieved smile of a woman gripping a sharpened blade. All palpable as the soft throbbing in my left thumb.

I put down knife and wood, and stood. Shavings cascaded onto the packed earth below. I stretched my aching back, spread my cramped fingers, and wondered how many hours I'd been hunched over, started to think about the class schedule, what might be next and what we'd do tomorrow and then the firelight caught my eye and I stopped thinking.

I watched the colors bob and shimmy on the wind. Tried to see beyond the yellows and oranges to find the blues and violets.

I exhaled. The cloud of my breath swirled away from me and disappeared.

I breathed in rain mist and cedar exhalations. I breathed in woodsmoke and sawdust. I breathed in sizzling venison. I breathed in wet wool and human musk.

Our bodies remember this. Bodies rendered from the bodies of those who came before, who sprang from those before them, back and back up tributaries to that mysterious river who dispatched us all. These ancient bodies pierced and porous, precarious bubbles flowing through all that is now. Deep down, we all remember this.

I picked up the green fire tending sticks and stirred the coals at the edge, drew them closer to the blaze. Pushed a smoldering log apart from others to give it air so it snapped into flame. Wood ignited, became heat, became the sweat on my brow, the flush in my cheeks, the fire in my body. My body, the tool to taste the earth.

And if we must return to this way of being?
What we'd lose is obvious. What we'd gain is harder to put into words, maybe because it flows from the time before words. The time before mind and body split, when body was mind.

Someone handed me a piece of roasted venison and I took it into my mouth, ground it down with my molars as warm juices slid down my throat. I swallowed, licked my fingers, and picked up steel knife and wooden spoon. They felt good in my hands. I raised the spoon, admired the colors emerging, the wavy patterns of the grain, like flame and shadow. I ran my thumb over it, felt the smooth curves where it was almost done and the rough edges that needed more work. I squatted by the fire, and carved. Blood-soaked shavings fell to the flames.

Fractions

¼

Another contraction starts. The shock of it catches your breath in your throat then releases it in choppy panting. Your fingers clench into fists, nails cutting into palms. Your jaw clamps together and grinds—squeaks bone on bone as eyes narrow to slits. Something tears at you, ripping you apart, and you struggle against it.

You are not in labor. But this feeling is born of love.

You throw the phone down. Turn on the radio. Pace the tile floor. You try not to think but the slicing pain finds you anyway. It comes in waves, though not in your abdomen, in your chest. The hollow somewhere beneath your ribcage. Glints of past and present slash at you like carnivorous claws.

Slash. Dad hits Mom. Mom locks herself in the bathroom to get away from him.

Slash. Stepdad shatters an empty glass of Dewar's against the wall and leaves, again.

Slash. Your own partner looks you in the eye and says trust me, it won't happen again. Then sneaks away to a mutual friend's bed.

This is love.

Slash. Your childhood friend, blood still drying on her forehead and under her nose, sits in a concrete jail cell wondering how her husband made this her fault. Wondering how she has become her mother.

Slash. The man she once loved is trying to take their daughter away. She wonders if he will hit her too.

Slash. Her daughter clings to Daddy and doesn't understand why Mommy went away.

½

You understand murder. You understand it as logically as you understand eating, sleeping, and fucking.

You imagine what you would do to him. Where you would punch, kick, slash to bring him down. How you would growl,

If you ever touch my friend again I will kill you.

How he would see in your eyes that you are telling the truth.

¾

You lie on your back on the earthen forest floor, legs splayed out and head propped against the smooth red skin of a cedar tree. The ground underneath you is cold, solid, yet rich with life. Not like tile. Not like concrete. Your fingers fondle the needles, twigs, and soil next to your hips and your lips curl into a smile.

It is dusk, and the first of the bats dart among the branches above. The October wind gusts through you and the cool freshness is a baptism. You open your mouth to it and breathe it in slowly, deeply, letting it fill you.

The thing that tries to tear you apart indoors can't touch you out here. Rage leaks out of you to decompose with the leaves. It evaporates in the wind. It is carried away on the wings of bats. It fades with the sunlight, and then there is only darkness.

There is no love here, so there is no breaking apart. There is only mending. What you absorb from the earth fills the cracks like tree sap. You are learning to be whole, by yourself.

Something moves in the blackness to your left, and your head darts in its direction. A stick snaps, then another. You leap to your haunches and squint to see but there is nothing but shadow and wind and somewhere, another animal that prefers solitude. You rock back against the cedar, feel its unyielding strength against your spine. Place your hands on your chest, press them against the bones of your ribcage. This is your heart racing.

$$4/4$$

Alone is not a sad word. Alone means safe, protected, free from love. Love is a word concerned only with the small lives of humans, not the greater earth. People think you are scared, bitter, fractured. Maybe so. But solitude means survival. It means you will never become your mother. You will never become your friend.

You can see they pity you. They cannot see you pity them.

They also cannot see that there is more to it than self-preservation. You know that remaining alone protects them from you. Alone means you will never become your fathers, your lover, your friend's husband. You know how easily you could be.

1

No, I am not in a relationship. No, you do not need to find somebody for me. No, I do not have kids. Yes, I do know what I am missing.

Journaling Purgatory

THEN

My coworker Mark asked me why I seemed to have endless energy and all I could tell him was that I was just so happy to be there. Happy to be living in a riverside cabin and working at the off-the-grid retreat center in the Oregon Cascades with no plans to leave. Excited to connect with the community of real people doing the same. And relieved to have space between me and my relationship with Lynn, back in the loud and crowded city where we were falling out of love.

So many new friends, new connections, new chemistry. Maybe it was the fire of the landscape working on me. Scalding mineral water bubbled up from the earth all around us. We soaked in it, breathed it in and sweat in it, ran it through pipes under the trails to the radiators in all the buildings. Visitors used to drink it, back in the 1930s when they believed all earthen waters must be healing. Never mind the lithium.

Skye asked me, "Do the fairies mess with you?" It was the sort of place people ask stuff like that. Not yet, I told him. But I wouldn't have been surprised.

Also? I was sort of in love with two new people – Caren and Bo. They both came into my life the week I got there, when I was missing Lynn and longing for someone new. They were both wild and enriched my life in different ways. Mostly physically. Caren was playful and fun. Bo was dark and brooding, mysterious. I thought about them constantly.

～

I sat alone next to a Manzanita shrub on a cliff partway up Devil's Peak and looked down at the Breitenbush valley. Trees, river, trees, then snow-heavy mountains as far as I could see. Nothing else. A hummingbird whizzed by my head, a buzzy blur that was gone by the time it entered my awareness. All of a sudden I was crying.

One minute I was excited to be there, sure it was the right choice and could see myself staying there for years. The next I was lonely and scared and didn't know why I was there. Why was I there? It was beautiful and perfect and exactly what I'd been looking for in a community, but…

I thought about Lynn constantly. I wasn't really there.

～

Was I actually sick almost a month? I must have been feverish for half of that, with coughing fits that went on so long I couldn't breathe and my throat and lungs on fire. An acupuncturist said the volcanic landscape was too fiery for me and it burned me out. Caren said it sounded like pneumonia and without medicine I was lucky I came out of it at all. I'd finally started to feel better but still so drained, depleted, raw, empty, and then my voice was gone. I couldn't make a sound. I've never lost my voice before. What was that about?

I missed Lynn, and I wanted to go home to the city. Caren was a fun diversion but had quickly moved on, acted like she never wanted me in the first place. Bo became increasingly intense, so needy, like a vampire. Even when I was sick she kept trying to take my clothes off and acted like a wounded pitbull when I pushed her away. But Bo was there and Lynn was not.

I sat by the river letting the sun hypnotize me with dancing diamonds on the surface. I could almost feel the warmth of approaching summer underneath the chill of lingering winter. It should have been perfect. A baby was born in the community and everyone was ecstatic. Instead, I was sad and weepy and anxious. And obsessing again. I thought about Lynn constantly. I wasn't really there.

∼

Spring blew in more energy, a spring fever. Wind gusted still naked cottonwoods until they creaked and cracked and the river swelled with snowmelt roared a steady storm. I tried to breathe it in and not let it sweep me away. At least I could take a deep breath again, and smell the river, the wet leaves on the ground, the conifers, maybe even the sunbeams themselves.

∼

Lynn and I got back together, for real, and I started to feel like myself again. I would move back to the city eventually so we could continue our life together. Bo moved to the city so I was free of that energy. I introduced Bo and Lynn, figured they could probably both use a new friend and that would keep Bo out of my hair. They'd probably get along great.

In the massage room, Mark told me his theory that we were all brought there for a purpose. To accomplish something, learn something, figure something out. After he said it, the wind picked up and blew the windows wide open and the candles danced, like a fairytale.

~

I sat on Devil's Peak. Shirt off, face to the sun. My skin was burning. Back in the city, I'd just learned, Lynn and Bo had become lovers. I was fine. I was fine.

~

I dreamt that Bo was scratching my face off while Lynn watched, laughing. I woke up screaming.

It was my birthday, and I went ahead with the party even though I had sores all over my face and in my mouth and I couldn't talk again and couldn't eat anymore. Lynn came to visit *me*, she said, though I knew Bo was also there, filling in for someone in the kitchen. Everyone came to the party and danced to the house music thumping from the city DJ and I pretended not to notice that Lynn and Bo left together and didn't come back.

~

Then, I left too. Packed up all my stuff and drove back to the city, then on to another state. I'm not sure I was ever really there.

Interlude

The first time I visited Breitenbush Hot Springs I was overcome with emotion, may have even cried a little. Something about the glacial-fed river and ancient moss-draped forest sheltering a community-run cedar cabin village, yurt-shaped meeting spaces, and creaky-floored dining hall said Home to me. That Home with a capital H that is simultaneously familiar and an unattainable ideal for which you will be forever homesick. Like the summer camps or the hippie communities my hippie mother exposed me to, the world of this healing arts retreat center was like a far-off dream I desperately wanted to get back. Yet when I first arrived, I had the strange feeling it had already slipped away.

I visited as a guest a few times before applying to work as a fill-in massage therapist. A year later I accepted a full-time year-round position in the community. I couldn't get enough of the clean mountain air scented with cedar and fir, always tinged with snowmelt even in the heat of summer. Or the roar of the river, so loud even inside the buildings that more than one massage client asked if I would turn the fan off. And the peaceful, smiling faces and the simplicity of mountain life, at least at first. For a while, it was the place of my dreams. Until they became nightmares. At Breitenbush everything was magnified, like the 180-degree water bubbling from the earth that had to be diluted with cold water before it reached the soaking pools. Connections blazed like lightning storms; lives melted together or sheared apart.

I cried when I left, too, though more from relief.

Years later, after spending time far from the Pacific Northwest, I returned to Oregon and returned to Breitenbush. Sometimes, to visit, other times to work as a fill-in employee. I was usually nervous getting there, often impatient to leave, but always glad I went. Despite sensing the ghosts of my tumultuous past in all the buildings and on every path, something in me knew the place wasn't done working on me. So I kept returning, and let it.

I returned in spring. I wandered in the Emerald Forest, somehow greener than the lowland Oregon forests ever are, from sword fern and moss-carpeted earth up moss and lichened trees to leafy needled canopy, all of it exhaling the sweetest woodland breath. I followed birdsong—hermit thrushes, hermit warblers, and ever-present ravens. I spent an afternoon watching two juvenile Douglas squirrels atop a cedar stump, wrestling and snuggling, grooming each other's yellow bellies and mousy faces. Little black eyes watched me back. I went out in the rain and floated face up in the far meadow hot spring pool under the willow overlooking the river, let the cool drops fall on my face and breasts while hot water caressed me from below. When I got too hot I climbed out and stood naked in the grass, steam rising from me.

I returned in summer. Lay naked next to a cold green pool called Devil's Hole, a deep eddy in Devil's Creek. Hot sun on my whole body, every nook and cranny, turning me from snow white to blood red in a matter of hours. Breeze caressed my hair everywhere making me feel charged and ecstatic, while hummingbirds whirred nearby seeking honeysuckle vines. When I got too hot I plunged in the creek, the icy shock of it making me gasp and gape. Then I air-dried, the wind and the sun having its way with me again. Heat and cold and heat and cold and sunburn and the whispering trees, cerulean sky, and long days of chartreuse light in the ethereal fairyland forest. Violet-green swallows darted above. Everything magnified, time stretched.

I returned in fall. Soaked in the near meadow pool under the crimson vine maple then jumped in the river and stayed in long enough for my head to spin and my lungs to balloon. I ran through the forest hopping over logs and ducking under branches, trailed a raccoon, collected Oregon Grape root to make a tincture, and kissed the smooth red bark of a yew tree. In the early evening I sat next to the river against the rock that holds the heat of the sun long after it sets, burning a red circle in my back. Bats darted and dove for insects over the water.

I returned in winter. In the darkest time of the year I moved between warm rooms and hot water as if in the earth's own womb. Tiny snowflakes defied gravity and floated around, floated up, kissing my neck and face with delicious coolness. Clumps of snow sloughed off pines and firs. I stood naked in the darkness and scrubbed icy snow on my steamy body. Heat to cold to heat to cold until my head throbbed, but I kept it up. Came back for more.

I returned again and again. To be cleansed, purified, purged of everything that came before. Purged of love, community, and utopia. Maybe even of my self.

NOW

It's been fifteen years since I first came here, though I'm not sure I was really here then. I am here now. Here for the quiet snowy forest by the river, for the hot water flowing from the earth, for individual trails and trees and birds, I've come to know and love.

And the people? The resident community members I wouldn't recognize anymore, and the other smiling visitors? They are around somewhere.

I woke at 4:30 this morning, refreshed. Snuggled in my sleeping bag and smiled until 5:00, when I finally gave in and got up. I was in the far meadow pool by 5:30, lazing under the willow listening to the roaring river and a great horned owl calling from the forest.

I ate alone again and haven't spoken to one person yet. I've managed to remain particularly solitary this visit, always eating at the two-top tables and not making eye contact. Nobody would dare sit across from me; why would they? I get there early and am leaving by the time the dining room fills. I smile and nod and am polite when appropriate, but so far have avoided small talk. That's not why I'm here.

After breakfast I crunched my way along the ski and snowshoe-packed trails into the forest, ducking under and pushing through leaning trees blocking the trail. The snow was three feet thick even on the stumps and bowed conifers and at times the trail was more like a tunnel. I felt small, like a mouse skittering through. Which was comforting, somehow. I tracked a snowshoe hare—giant back feet. And red fox—dainty steps like a cat. I like to think of them out here with me, somewhere. Even blanketed in snow, this forest is so familiar, so comfortable. I know it better than I did when I lived here, from my time spent learning, teaching, and restoring other Northwest forests. Western redcedar, Douglas fir, grand fir. Vine maple, Oregon grape, sword fern. Rivers braiding off sections of forest, both river and forest different every year.

But more than that, I know these trails. Know these particular trees and shrubs, these holey snags, this mountain air, and these rivers. Oh, I know, a river is just individual water droplets rushing away to somewhere else, never the same. That's true, but the Breitenbush River, and its tributary Devil's Creek, they are unified entities. Not always leaving, always arriving, always here. That is also true.

The ravens were chatty today, singing, giving speeches. One raven perched directly above me, pontificating. Two water droplet notes sung to the sky and then two hunched-shoulder shimmy-chortles, on repeat. It was so comical and delightful and probably not for my benefit, but I couldn't see any other ravens nearby just then. Soon I was grinning and giggling out loud, but he just kept it up. *Toot toot, chuckle chuckle.* I found a feather already, last night in the dark. The iridescent sheen. It was near the place where one winter I watched a raven making snow angels. Which are so much better than human ones, because ravens have real wings.

Sometimes it feels as if the ravens are the only real life here. The humans seem unreal, far away from me. I watch them from the fringes as if watching a play. They reenact the same dramas, fight the same demons. I can see my past self there too.

Or maybe I am the one who is no longer real, a ghost moving between forest and hot water, watching the birds who live in between. A shaman here once told me that ghosts are people who've died and haven't crossed over, and are lonely being invisible. Did some part of me die here, back then? Should I be lonely? I'm not. I have so many old friends here. Friends of earth, air, fire, and water. I feel safe, and just so, happy. Ecstatic even. From death, rebirth.

It's the last day of the year, and I spent the evening soaking alone in the near meadow pool under the vine maple. I sat back near where the heat trickles out of the earth, feeling cold kisses on my face that must have been snowflakes though I couldn't see them in the darkness, and I looked out to where stars would be on a clear night.

Once I was sufficiently cooked I made my way toward the river. I moved in the shadows, no flashlight, no moon. I don't need them anymore, not here. I shrank from the path lights, hid from the few passersby. When someone swept a flashlight my way I ducked into the shadow of a fir tree. After they'd gone I moved out into the open field to the labyrinth. In clouded blackness I could just make out the stone borders —snowy mounds above the darker earth, like the subtle ridges of a fingerprint. I walked the path, in and out, forward and back, around and around. Spiraled between the places I'd been and the places I've yet to be. Stumbled some, but mostly walked steadily in the darkness. I found the center. I am here.

Pilgrim

I didn't go there to swim. Not that I wouldn't, sometimes, if the inland heat managed to beat out the cooling coastal fog and the waves didn't appear too menacing. I also wasn't there to work on my tan, or more accurately, freckles and burn, as the chill breeze off the Pacific would keep me more covered up than not.

My east coast friends wouldn't understand this. Back east on the beaches of my youth—Rhode Island's Watch Hill or Misquamicut, Cape Cod's Provincetown, or Long Island Sound's Hammonasset—the sweltering heat followed you to the shore and even into the Atlantic, which warmed to tepid. Baby oiled bikinied bodies lined the scorching sand like strips of bacon in a deep fryer, so that you had to plan your route from your towel into the water around wrists and feet, beer coolers and umbrellas, and dogs and children digging to China. You went there for the fun of floating in the warm salted sea. You went there for a change of scenery in the doldrums of August. Maybe you went there to be seen, to flirt with friends or strangers. You went there because it's just what was done. You sat in traffic with your family, or once you were old enough, your friends, with the A/C blasting and heat waves rising off the pavement in the long lines of cars descending from cities and suburbs and you did so again on the way home, stopping, perhaps, for clam strips or fried calamari, lobstah rolls or clam chowdah. Then, of course, ice cream. It's just what you did.

I went to Cannon Beach alone. Drove west instead of east, over the coast range mountains then south away from kitschy commercial Seaside to quaint charming Cannon Beach. I parked in the tiny lot next to the public bathrooms, where somehow there was usually a spot left for me even on summer weekends when cars inched around the town loop ready to rev into any vacant space. At some point in my visit I would wander into shops, buy a book from an author I'd never heard of from the Cannon Beach Bookstore, and get halibut fish tacos at the Ecola Fish Market. Then, of course, ice cream. But I wasn't there for the town.

West, up second street to the end of the road and the top of the stairs to the view that once hit me like a tourist reaching mecca, but now greets me as the deep comfort of homecoming. There, where the sand somehow spills up concrete stairs and onto the blacktop, the bottleneck portal where the giddy beachbound remove shoes and unleash dogs and children, where those returning up the stairs try and fail at reigning in dogs and children and shoes and hair, all animals windblown and sand-laden and smiling anyway, and where rubberneckers in city clothes lean out over the metal railing, snapping pictures and making mental notes to stop there longer, next time.

Sandals off and tucked into the outer pocket of my

backpack, I slalomed around families, couples, and dogs, down, around, and down onto soft sand. Then pushed on away from the crowd, away from that liminal coming-and-going place and out into the open, toward the roar of the mighty Pacific. Only then—deep breath—did I stop and take it all in.

Like a mental checklist, I noted all the component parts, always there, but always slightly changed from last time, and would change again by the time I left later that day. It had been hot and dry that particular August, so the sand was especially warm and soft between my toes. Never scorching, just comfortably warm, like heated flooring. The tide was in, so the ocean's roar was closer, but still far enough so that the sound was more rhythmic rumbling than deafening crashing, and still acres of dry sand the color of fresh-baked bread before the darker gray wet stretched gleaming toward the surf. Plenty of space for everyone to disburse, to fade into the white noise.

To the north, Ecola creek—ecola from the Chinook word *ehkoli*, meaning whale—flowed in from stable earthen banks in town to haphazard changeable meandering across the beach to reach the ocean, sloughing off sand at one edge then the other and playing tug-o-war with fresh and saltwater in the cyclic tides. In the distance beyond the creek, beyond the first grassy dunes, above the houses on the bluffs, Ecola State Park's cliffs sketched a Japanese ink painting of crooked Zen pines and austere old-growth Sitka spruces.

To the south stood the monolith of Cannon Beach,

Haystack Rock. Aptly (if not creatively) named for its shape, a giant-sized 235-foot stack of igneous basalt once an outcrop of mainland now stood separate, an island in high tide. In low tide still set apart by a jeweled necklace of tide pools with ruby and amethyst starfish, sea urchins, and anemones.

Relatively symmetrical, Haystack Rock looked tidy and contained from afar. A colonial farmer's job well done, period. Just a big, inanimate rock. But I and an annual thousand other gawkers knew differently. Later I would walk closer, peer through binoculars, and I'd see, remember—that mountain was alive. Green with hardy ground covers on any remotely horizontal surface, splattered with white from the orbit of swirling of birds above. Tufted puffins, common murres, pigeon guillemots, and auklets communed with the less exotic terns and gulls, coming in to rest, roost, nest on cliffs safe from ground predators—if not aerial—then lifting off again in shifts, locals or tourists in search of seafood. At some point I would take a picture, though I have dozens, though I know pictures will never capture the scale, the animation, the natal stench of the living breathing landscape that must have boasted a better name, once, before Lewis and Clark with their tame dead words of long-tamed dead places and people, a name worthy of a living landscape.

Monolith in view, I walked south. Kept closer to the dunes, seeking just the right driftwood log to set up shop for the day. No people or dogs camped out within speaking distance—that's a no-brainer—and far enough away from both the water and subtle trails through dune grasses up to other dead-end roads so that nobody would walk close to me. I wasn't looking for total peace and quiet, not the solitude of a dark forest trail on a rainy weekday. I just wanted all that action farther from me, where I could appreciate it.

And I found it, the perfect driftwood log. Still more tree than log, this skeleton of a giant had the buttressed base of a cedar, nubby roots now reaching up to the sky, the length of three park benches and even a slight curl at the bottom to create a windbreak. Oriented parallel to the shore so that if I chose to sit up against it I would face the ocean. Flattened on top so that I might sit up there out of the sand if I chose, or just use it as a table for my things, which I laid out to stake my claim. Binoculars, journal, and book on the table. Backpack with water bottle stashed below leaning against it in the shade. Towel spread in front, perpendicular.

Next order of business, remove my hooded sweatshirt and lie down in tank top and shorts. Snuggle down on my belly out of the breeze and in to the warmth through my towel, molding the very earth to my own body and feeling the sun on bare limbs. The delicious heat below and above, serotonin endorphin heat all around that instantly had me sighing and grinning. Just, lying on the ground. Sighing and grinning, every time.

One cheek to the earth, the other to the sky, sounds funneled in to the ear of the driftwood log curled around me then my own ear exposed. Then back down through my other ear into the earth.

I heard the waves rolling in like a bass drum roll, advancing up the beach, closer, louder, then retreating again. And again. This most ancient, original ebb and flow, the very earth breathing. Without intention, my own inhales and exhales lengthened and stretched, syncing with the waves.

All other sounds softened when added to this bass rhythm, filtered through my ears to the sand. Squeaks of young children running toward and away from the water like novice sanderlings, and a brave two or three older ones yelping in the waves despite themselves as the cold had its way with them. Yips of dogs in ecstatic glee at so much space to run and run and their humans tossing Frisbees and balls and Kongs and *ohmygoodness please please please just throw it again*. Caws of crows and peals of gulls (who may finally, rightly be called seagulls again) discussing lunch plans, rejoicing that humans oblivious to birds will leave bags unattended and coolers open and won't remember these residents' boldness until it's too late.

Sighing and grinning, I loved them all.

Children, dogs, birds, waves, all soft and subtle, the hummed mantra of Cannon Beach. I was inside and apart from the sounds, as I was inside and apart from everything that came before the humming now. From the New England beaches of my youth. From my father who came to this beach as a child on summer vacations, swimming lessons in the frigid Ecola creek. From my grandfather, the Portland native who summered here as a youth and retired here as an elder, gin and tonics on a creaky porch. And from my great grandfather, a Portland to Cannon Beach transplant whose cottage on Adams Street would have been walking distance from where I lay. The Cannon Beach of my forefathers was part of the hum too. Maybe, I went there because of them.

I sat up and looked out at the land of my forefathers, then the waters beyond. Back against the log, feet off the sides of my towel dug into the warm yellow sand, I looked out at the blue. Sunny days dealt in primary colors, a child's drawing of a seascape. One could draw that whole scene with a basic box of Crayolas and simple shapes. A few green tufts on the rounded hills behind me, the foreground of the picture. Light yellow—don't press down with the crayon—filling in the bottom of the paper up to a solid line where blue begins. An inch of dark blue—press down hard; if you break the crayon, no matter—leaving some thin strips without color for the froth of the waves. Off in the distance on the left side of the paper, a brown haystack with a green top. Go ahead, add some bird chevrons above. Just a little squiggle like a symmetrical checkmark, you remember. Pick up the blue again, and with a lighter touch, fill in the sky. Finally, a dark yellow orb near the top right corner. Don't forget the rays shining down on all of it. Perfect.

On a cloudy day, you'd need many more colors. A professional artist's palette of grays, blues, purples, opalescent pink and yellow, more greens and silver and black and who are you kidding, more colors than they make in the most extensive set of pastels and you may as well not try because you couldn't pull it off anyway.

On a cloudy day, when a gull's cry turns melancholy and the cruise ship in the distance morphs into an ancient fishing vessel, I can almost remember the shores of my ancestors before the Cannon Beach generations. Before the New England generations. Instead of salal and salmonberry thickets and misted spruce cliffs—bracken lowlands and craggy oak highlands. Peat bogs and heather moorland. Shrubby juniper and flowering azalea. Both places? Moss and fern-laced. Upland lakes and wildflower meadows. Host to salmon and seal, eagle and deer.

My roots in the British Isles are thick, matted, and ancient. Maybe, even, deep enough to be called indigenous. I wonder how it might feel to know that rootedness, that home of the old ones. Maybe my New England family came to coastal Oregon seeking that ancient home, not in any conscious way, but from some subtle tug that made this place feel most right on this continent, right in the earliest and deepest sense of the word.

Here, we'll always be pilgrims. And like childhood stories of the Pilgrims in the East, we've too often distorted or erased the Indians who came first. For thousands of years before my family, tens of thousands even, Cannon Beach was home to Chinookan tribes of the lower Columbia River. Clatsop and Chinook people and their foremothers and fathers were the first humans to stare out at the seabound hill swirling with birds, to watch the living creek slither through golden sand to meet the sea, and to listen to and breathe with the ocean until their breath was the same. I would like to know their stories of this place before we named it for a cold steel weapon of war, their stories that must have stretched on to where the sky meets the sea. Speaking their names, as I know them, is the least I can do, though it's not enough.

A gust of chill wind made me lay back down on my towel, cheek to the earth, hand reached out to sift sand through my fingers. It was always softer than I remembered it, and looking more closely I could see it wasn't yellow at all. Cannon Beach sand contains all the colors of granite, every shade of white, gray, pink, tan, gold, sparkling mica grains, blowing over me. Onto my towel, into my tangled hair, and sticking to my sunscreen smeared arms. That felt right.

Warm again on the earth behind my driftwood windbreak, I focused out and watched the sand grains blow over one another, a looser, drier top layer moving over a more solid base layer but all of it changeable, shifting and crumbling. Sand as far as the eye could see. Mesmerizing, beautiful, but devoid of life. Just tiny little rocks.

If it weren't for the hum of the waves I could almost imagine myself marooned in a desert wasteland. Not the rich deserts of this continent host to blooming cacti and a whole menagerie of skittering reptiles and colorful birds. Rather, the inert deserts of my colonialist collective unconscious. Places of exile where a rootless patriarchal monotheism first swirled into being and blew over my forefathers like a storm. Where earth and body were desacralized and the great mystery took shape as a man and He left the earth to some otherworld On High. Sandblind and rootless, those ancestors held their feeling of exile long after leaving the desert, even into the lush, fertile landscapes of the northern isles. Even west over the ocean to new shores, where they/we blew over this continent like a storm and continue to spread even now, sandblind and rootless, bulldozing life and actualizing the wastelands in our hearts.

Enough.

I stood, lay my backpack and shoes on my towel so it wouldn't blow away, and walked toward the water. I arced a wide path around three gulls who stood facing the wind, and noticed in the distance others floating on the water or hovering just above, all oriented the same way, like a single organism. On the bluffs to the south crooked pine trees stood defiantly on the cliff edge, they too all oriented the same as if arms reaching out toward the sea, and I knew that just over those hills old growth Sitka spruce spread licorice fern arms wide to shield sword ferns and wrens below. Later, walking in that forest, I would watch a poison-orange rough-skinned newt waddle across the trail and listen to ravens sing out staccato duets high above. The rich coastal landscape of Cannon Beach's first people was undeniably changed and still changing, but it still lived and breathed, where it could. Salmon and shellfish, salmonberries and nettles, cattails and miner's lettuce. Deer, elk, otter, beaver, and bear. Cedar trees, this land's Tree of Life.

At the water's edge, I looked down to find a whole sand dollar shell. Pale creamy white like the sand, but made of calcium, not silica. The skeleton from a living animal, not a broken rock. An abiotic piece, yes, but once an integral part of a breathing, moving, eating, reproducing being. Sand holds their memories too.

I picked up the skeleton, traced the five-pointed star inside the circle. Like the five-pointed star of a starfish, the inside of a halved apple, a eucalyptus seed pod, a thousand flowers, meaningful symbols in multiple religions and belief systems older than religion, and childish doodles. We've all been seeing stars for a long, long time. Too often, I think, we cling to the symbol and forget the world we plucked it from. This world, this breathing, moving, living world.

I walked the final few feet toward the surf and into the cold blue. Gave the skeleton back to the ocean and stood to look out. Blowing sand behind me, I focused on the complex blue palette in front of me as it shifted and quaked, rose and fell. I tried to imagine all the lives lived in or from the inscrutable seascape.

The tide was coming in, ocean rising over sand, flowing up Ecola creek, as the moon waxed above, as my body prepared to bleed. I breathed with the waves, let the noise fill my ears, let the water wash over my toes, then feet, then ankles. I closed my eyes and let the hum fill me, strained to hear the whispers older than my forefathers, older than the pilgrims, even older than the Indians. The ultimate wildness, unfathomable but undeniably present. More mother than father, the source of the earth-centered richness of watery places of indigenous peoples everywhere. The oldest spirituality not of alienation, but of belonging. I opened my eyes. Blowing sands behind me, I faced the living sea. This, I believe, is why I came.

I turned south and aimed for Haystack rock. Squinted to see the corona of birds circling above. Eyes on the birds, feet in the water, I walked.

Ergo Sum

You three have medical cards, right?

My friends and I exchanged glances. How does it go in Canada?

The shop attendant cued us again. *You have medical cards, right?* Nod. Exaggerated nod.

Yes yes, of course we did. Sure.

And then, just like that, we bought a little marijuana. Just enough to roll a couple joints, since we'd have to use it up before we crossed back over the border. Back then the U.S. was still a dozen years from all but the strictest medical use.

You ladies want to try something special, on the house?

Why not? We followed the attendant to the back of the shop where he opened a door into a dark room so hazy with pot smoke I felt high immediately.

As my eyes adjusted through the murky fog I could see several smiling men sitting in an assortment of cushioned easy chairs and wooden kitchen chairs, all oriented toward one man who held a small vial of a waxy-looking amber paste. On a side table lay a six-inch-long clear glass tube, a lighter, and a butter knife.

We were three generally well-behaved and law-abiding women on a thirtieth birthday outing to Vancouver, B.C. and we were now surrounded by strange men in a dim storeroom that looked exactly the way I imagined a crack den. Probably I should have been freaking out right about then. But, I wasn't. Partly because it was Canada, and I have the bias that they are more civilized there. More mature, more decent, less likely to cling to guns like teddybears, ask their God to bless their country yet deny universal healthcare, or vote a fascist megalomaniac into office, for example. But also, it was a marijuana shop; everything and everyone reeked with the sweet earthy musk of Cannabis. Cannabis is not a lab-cooked drug of violence, but a soil-grown plant of peace. Languid, slothful peace.

The host tipped his head toward the empty chairs closest to him and got right to business. *This is Cannabis butter, 99% pure THC.*

Cool. Must be like the infused butter you can use for brownies. Mmmm, brownies.

I doubted pot butter could have such a highly concentrated THC content but figured they were showing off for the foreigners. No harm in that, and no harm in taking one hit.

I would learn later that this wasn't butter, it was "budder," also known as Cannabis wax or BHO—Butane Hash Oil—an extremely potent chemical extract. 99% was still probably an exaggeration. But maybe not.

Mel, the self-proclaimed pothead of our threesome, went first. Our host dabbed the oily resin onto the tip of the knife, clicked the Bic lighter, and held the flame to it. She took up the glass pipe, sucked up the smoke, coughed a little, said *Whoooa*. Her eyes widened. *Wooow*. She sat back and grinned. I looked at Lynn, who shook her head no. My turn then.

I wasn't much of a pot smoker but when I did smoke the dried sage-green flowerbuds, I liked the way I felt. Feel. I relax instantly. Anxieties and racing thoughts wane, and heightened awareness makes old things new again. Maybe I am more likely to forget some things, but I am also more likely to remember others. A task that had fallen off my radar will suddenly reappear in my thoughts. I'll notice how dirty my windows are with the sun streaming through, or have the sudden realization that I haven't heard the varied thrushes for a while and that they must have moved back up into the mountains for summer.

Unlike alcohol which deadens my awareness, makes me foggy, slow, sad, or stupid, a single hit of marijuana can clear away the fog, leaving me sunnier, maybe with a few puffy white clouds. Still me, just more easygoing. Less edgy. Like after an afternoon nap and a hot fudge sundae. And after a couple hours or when waking up the next day, I am back to my regular self again. No hangover, no residue. Just freshly me.

The only other drugs I'd tried were mushrooms, a few times, and acid, once. Mushrooms were a little like pot, magnified to a place where I and the world were recognizable though decidedly altered, *Alice in Wonderland* style. Everything was a little off, which could be fascinating or hysterically silly one moment and uncomfortably unsettling the next. Nothing to freak out about; I was always aware enough to remind myself that I was just "shrooming" and it would wear off. Still, mushrooms were the drugs of my more reckless youth, and I felt no desire to ingest them again.

    I only did acid because I was twenty-one, my closest friends were doing it too, and we'd locked ourselves in one of their houses when parents were away so we would be less likely to get ourselves arrested or killed or lose our minds. And even though I heard my friends talking about me as if I wasn't there deciding who would knock me out if I started losing my shit because I was the most mentally unstable, I managed to keep it together. At least I think I did. I'd describe the experience to you if I could but the me writing this is entirely unable to access the me on acid. I can't even see her from the outside. I do remember some of how we passed the time, mainly because I remember discussing it the next day. For a long time (I think) we listened to the soundtrack from *The Doors* movie which in addition to some of the best Doors music includes some other crazy-making songs like a full operatic version of O Fortuna from Carmina Burana. We also sat around in a circle petting the black cat, took turns looking at ourselves in the mirror because we'd heard that was supposed to be cool, passed a Tetris Gameboy back and forth, made toast just to look at but not ingest, and tried not to vomit. So basically, we didn't do much of anything. Which I'm pretty sure was all I would have been able to handle. Eventually the two of us left awake lay on the couch passing the remote control back and forth, though I can't tell you what was on. I can't tell you if it was fun. *I was gone.* I don't know who was in my body during that time, maybe no one, but it definitely wasn't me. I don't regret the experience, but I would never do it again. I also don't plan to try any harder drugs. A few puffs of marijuana now and then is quite enough, thank you very much.

I exhaled, emptying my lungs. Then took the glass tube from Mel, curled my lips around it and as soon as the flame met the knife I sucked in the sweet smoke until I felt full to bursting.

Deep inside me, flames ignited. Figurative flames, probably. But maybe not.

I coughed out clouds of smoke, the searing burn traveling backward from lungs up trachea to throat, which began to tighten and constrict, shrinking like plastic thrown to the fire. I couldn't breathe. I wheezed and hacked and clawed at my throat to release whatever demon was squeezing me, but I couldn't see it. Couldn't see anything anymore, my vision gone dark.

Someone said, *it's time to go,* and we were back out on the street. Lynn at one elbow, Mel at the other, we walked. I coughed and sucked in air and eventually, my throat relaxed some. The searing eased to a singe. I would have been embarrassed at my amateur coughing fit, except...

How do you feel?

I couldn't answer. Couldn't speak the words. They were there, in my head. *I* was there in my head, but I couldn't remember how to get out. The complicated combination of the right sounds with the right movements of cheeks, tongue, and lips was too much. My legs moved as they pulled me along but I was pretty sure I wouldn't be able to do that for much longer. I still couldn't see, though my eyes were open. My brain seemed to have quit making sense of anything my eyes picked up, so nothing was out there. Not darkness, just, nothing.

Do you want to go out to eat? Should we go find some music?

I managed to half shake my head and get out the "N" sound. They got the picture and took me back to the bed and breakfast where we were staying. Lynn sat me on the couch and turned on the TV, thinking I could veg out there until the drug wore off. *Do you want to watch this?* She didn't know I couldn't see the television and I couldn't answer, so she put the remote in my lap and went to hang out with Mel, who was evidently speaking, moving, and seeing like she normally did. Or like she did when she was more stoned than she'd ever been in her life, as she would explain later. Still, nothing more than extremely high.

I was something else. I was in trouble. I was locked inside my body with no means of expression. Was this what it felt like to be severely autistic? Or worse, catatonic? Comatose? What if I never got out again? My breath came faster, my throat threatened to narrow again. I had to calm down. I found my hands, pressed the acupressure points I remembered from a

Shiatsu class that were supposed to help with panic. I pressed, dug my nails into my palms, as much just to feel the body out there and it helped, I think. It was the only thing I could do, and I wasn't sure I would be able to do that much longer either. But my thoughts—they were working. So I started a mantra. *It's only pot. You can't overdose on marijuana. Nobody dies from THC. Time will pass, and it will wear off.*

I believed it.

It's only pot (except it wasn't; it was Butane Hash Oil.)

You can't overdose on marijuana (but from chemical extracts made from marijuana you can lose consciousness, or worse.)

Nobody dies from THC (but BHO can retain a butane residue which acts as a neurotoxin, which sure as hell can kill you, or maybe just leave you locked inside your useless body forever and ever.)

The fire had spread to my stomach, and suddenly I was retching. Still sitting where they left me on the edge of the couch I threw up Cuban food from lunch and pastries from breakfast and then acid bile and though Lynn's voice was next to me begging me to go to the bathroom to puke in the toilet, her hand on my back pushing me, I knew I couldn't walk anymore. This body I was in, this body covered in vomit was no different than the couch, the room, the earth. I was only a voice. A voice in the darkness that could only say, *Time will pass. It will wear off.*

I had been locked inside myself before. Once in a long while during times of stress or sleep deprivation I experience sleep paralysis: the experience of consciously waking up from sleep while being unable to wake up the physical body. I remember the first time vividly. One afternoon during my junior year of college, in the four-bedroom duplex I shared with three friends at the University of Virginia, I was overtired and recovering from partying too much the night before so I decided to take a nap. Nobody else was home so I chose to snooze on the couch instead of climbing up to my loft bed in my tiny room. I slept quickly, hard, deeply, and later awoke with a start as if from some internal dream or external noise and it was as if I'd fallen back into my body from far away, plunk, and I was wide awake. Rigid on my back, I was aware of my surroundings, could see the room, hear the cars whizzing by on Jefferson Park Avenue below but I couldn't get up. And I couldn't make a noise. A leaden blanket pressed me down, compressed my chest. I was petrified.

I started to scream. Inside. I started to writhe, and kick, and punch, and fight, and though my body didn't move, my brain was sending signals somewhere, I could feel them, could feel the exertion of my body, my vocal cords, the blood pulsing through my veins. And eventually, it worked. I broke through the surface, swam back to myself, jolted back into my body as if shocked with electrodes. Though it seemed painfully slow, it probably took less than a minute until I was sitting upright, eyes wide, panting.

This was different. I was farther away somehow, all connections with my body now gone, as if they were never there in the first place. I could no longer find my hands or legs, couldn't locate my vocal cords. The body may still have been there, but it was no longer mine. I was vaguely aware of someone nearby cleaning up my mess, but that may as well have been in another room. Or maybe I was in another room. I was no longer locked inside my body; I was locked out.

What made sleep paralysis so terrifying was that I was perfectly aware of everything, decidedly present in time and space, just unable to move. But under the influence of this chemical or its byproduct, I'm not sure where *I* was anymore. I existed in another realm, separate from the physical. Not on a couch, in a room, in a city, on the earth. Somewhere else. It was scary, yes, but it was more of a philosophical sort of fear. Existential. There was nothing to fight, and no way to fight it. Only my internal voice remained.

Was this death? Had I died?

There was nothing to do but submit.

So.

This is who I am. This is my very essence, 99% pure. I am not my body. I am not any of the roles I play, my jobs, my actions, my environment. My past, my family, my relationships. Not even my passions, my anxieties, or my rage. Those are all of the world, but I exist outside of all that. I am only this voice. These words.

Is that so terrible?

In that realm outside of time and space, it wasn't terrible at all. Without everything else, all the complicated stuff of a human life, I still had me. And, surprisingly, I was comfortable with that. My voice, my consciousness, was home.

I. Am. That was the only truth, and that wasn't so terrible.

Descartes was right. *Cogito ergo sum.* The rest is superfluous.

I wasn't scared anymore. I now understood that no matter what happened out there, no matter what I experienced (or didn't), no matter what anyone did to me (or didn't), nothing could change this. Nothing could steal this from me. In the deepest sense of the word, *I* was SAFE. Always had been, and always would be.

If it sounds like a religious experience, it wasn't. Though I had had such musings before and would have them again, at the time I had no thought of my soul or spirit. My personal beliefs have always been fuzzy regarding such things, and though at my more fanciful times I like to believe I have a higher self that came before this life and will go on after it, this didn't feel like that. I also didn't feel any other presence outside of my self, didn't glimpse god or goddess or feel a benevolent force comforting me or any of that. In fact I felt more alone than I ever have in my whole life. I felt only my own consciousness, a disembodied psyche as Jung might have told it, and there was nothing high and mighty about it. And yet, it felt more real, more true than any experience of the world ever had. That's what made it home—what made it okay.

I am.

I am.

I am.

And then, slowly, from very far away, the world began to return. Not through one sense at a time but all together, as if someone turned a master dial in tiny increments. I breathed and felt my lungs and chest expand against the bucket Lynn had placed in my lap. Soft yellow lamps glowed on crimson Victorian furniture and a navy Oriental rug. The TV was dark now, as was the view out the window. The city was quiet. I felt my heart beating, savored my breath, the warmth of my body, the dampness of my hair where someone had washed it, the smell of Lysol, and even the sour taste in my mouth.

So. This was the world.

For a while, I just watched. Listened. Smelled, felt, and tasted. For seconds, minutes, maybe an hour, that was enough. Then, when I knew I could, I shifted my arm to grip the bucket and move it to the floor. I tightened my stomach muscles to move my torso forward out of my slouch to sit up straight, placed my feet on the rug.

I sat like that for more seconds, minutes, maybe an hour, until Lynn came in and looked at me. I looked at her. Curly brown hair, dark Italian eyes crinkled with worry, a red long-sleeved shirt, and plaid flannel pajama bottoms. She crossed her arms and watched me silently, expectantly.

I opened my mouth, tried my voice. *I'm tired. I'm going to go to bed now.* She came to me, helped me stand, and walked with me into the bedroom. Outside a song sparrow sang in the pre-dawn twilight. I sat down on the bed, got under the covers, and slept.

When I woke it was midday. My body felt wrecked, depleted, but not painful. As if I'd performed the workout of my life, as if I'd danced all night, no, for several days and nights together without stopping. I had no headache, wasn't nauseous or hungover as after heavy drinking. Just, worn out, and maybe a little cloudy. Quite hungry. And, I realized, still extremely stoned.

For the next two days in Vancouver and a third back in Portland, I was stoned. I wasn't always aware of it, but in that typical stoner double-take I would occasionally stop what I was doing and wonder, *am I still high? Oh yeah, I'm totally high.* The world just wasn't quite what it had been. Everything felt slightly off, surreal. And overstimulating in a way it hadn't been before that made me want to crawl back inside myself where everything was turned down and I could be by myself again. It wasn't fun, but it wasn't miserable either. It was just unsettling. Like a glaring spotlight you can't turn off or the whine of a mosquito in your ear. I was pretty sure it would pass. At least I hoped it would pass.

One day I stepped back and asked again, *am I still high?* And the answer was, *I don't think so. No.*

But I'm not so sure the baselines of before and after were the same, nor whether the difference between high and not high is ever clear. At the extreme ends of the spectrum, of course, yes. But consciousness is a messy thing, especially when confounded by all manner of chemical and environmental factors, steady streams of inputs that pour over us from all directions, as long as we are awake. Not drugs, the world. Hot sun on bare skin after a dip in an icy river, the rumble of thunder on a humid afternoon, flames dancing in the darkness. The smell of coffee brewing, onions sautéing in a skillet, or the Thanksgiving turkey in the oven, almost ready. A lover's arms around you pulling you close, an ex-lover's cold shoulder, a fallen child screaming in pain.

As long as we are awake, for most of us, most of the time, the world is out there, making itself known. And we are here in it, with the most mysterious, most wondrous, most confusing gift of all, the simple ability to notice.

I forget sometimes, as we all do. Too many people around or too much input deadens my awareness until I lose my sense of self. My inner voice goes away, checks out. No voice inside? No world outside. I'm not talking about extreme cases from trauma. Just everyday human experiences.

I used to lead large volunteer groups in tree planting projects. Most Saturdays I spent from 8 a.m. to 1 p.m. managing a dozen crew leaders and up to a couple hundred general volunteers in planting hundreds to several thousand seedling trees and shrubs. After one demonstration I rarely ever planted anything myself, but ran around blackberry thatched hillsides or soggy marshes answering questions and fixing mistakes and offering assistance and finding forgotten plants and redirecting misbehaving children and encouraging tired adults and troubleshooting unforeseen complications. At the end of it all, every weekend, I had overseen the beginning or continuation of a restored forest that would improve wildlife habitat, help clean the water, and bring more human happiness to my chosen corner of the world. Good, meaningful, important work, right?

It was. I was proud of my job. And yet, I was also inexplicably anxious, edgy, even angry. At the end of a workday, which—when you factored in project setup and cleanup—would often clock in at ten hours, I would come out of it as if coming off a drug. Not a happy drug. The sort of drug that obliterated everything I was. I would come out of it saying, *what just happened? Where was I?*

Yes, I'm an introvert. Obviously. But I'm talking about more than just being drained by other people. I was physically and emotionally tired afterward, yes. But during, I was often just gone. On some sort of autopilot, an automaton, a drone. Where did *I* go?

Developmental psychology teaches us that humans gain self-awareness by age two. This is the basic awareness of self as distinct from others, as distinct from the world. A red dot on a toddler's nose that when seen in a mirror makes her reach up and touch her own nose rather than the nose in the mirror.

Multiple studies beginning in 1970 with Gordon Gallup and his chimps have taught us that other animals can share this sort of visual self-awareness. And not just primates. Dolphins. Magpies. This is simple self-recognition. Just, *I am*. So what about the *I think* part of the equation? What about thinking *about* the fact that I am?

In 2003 Phillippe Rochat of Emory University identified five distinct levels of self-awareness. The first level is the basic *I am* of self-recognition. Only when we get up to level five are we thinking about that. Rochat describes this level as "meta self-awareness", awareness of the self from the first person *and* the third person. That ability to recognize and evaluate your self as if from the outside. What I resonate with most in Rochat's paper is a statement he makes in his conclusion, not about our development as children, but our existence throughout our lives:

"As adults, we are constantly oscillating in our levels of awareness: from dreaming or losing awareness about ourselves during sleep, to being highly self-conscious in public circumstances or in a state of confusion and dissociation as we immerse ourselves in movies or novels. In fact, each of these oscillating states of self-awareness can be construed as constant transition between the 5 levels emerging early in life." [9]

Confusion and dissociation from movies and novels? Definitely. I willingly allow that to happen and enjoy the journey, then enjoy returning to myself afterward to find I am new or changed from the experience. Confusion and dissociation from getting lost in the human world, engaging with too many people, or in over-stimulating environments? That seems beyond my control. Resurfacing after those experiences, wondering what just happened and where I'd gone—that's more uncomfortable, that's scarier even than being a disembodied psyche. Without my psyche, I'm just a body. Any body. Nobody.

That voice inside? It's home. I like to check in with it regularly. *Am I awake? Am I happy? Am I hiding from emotional connection, again? Am I terrified? I am?* That voice reminds me I am living.

In situations where I am able to remain present, the voice checks in with me too. Clears its throat, nudges my arm, pulls me outside myself to say *Look! Listen! This is beauty. This is grace.* Or, *this is scary. This is important. Remember this.* More than any of my bodily senses, that voice is what allows me to wholly, intimately, inhabit the world.

For my thirty-ninth birthday, I spent three days on my own camping in a red rock canyon outside of Sedona Arizona. For three days I wandered—up and down one foothill, then up and down another on the opposite side of the valley. Along one side of the canyon, then back along the other. I sat on one sandy creek bank looking across the water to where the next day I would lay on smooth sandstone on the other side, watching a yellow swallowtail butterfly taste the red mud. The sparse desert landscape needed no trails, and I was free to follow birdsongs, wildflowers, and sycamore trees in lazy spirals. I collected red dust and yellow grass seed in the webbing of my sandals. Sat in vortex sites demarcated by stone circles, watching red ants and yellow birds. Time slowed. I slowed. Even my heart's pace, which I knew because I even attended to that. I saw, heard, felt, smelled, and tasted everything, and attended to all of it. For three days I didn't do much of anything. And yet I was very busy.

The final day found me sitting on top of a red rock ridge, sun hot on my arms and neck, earth hot under my bare feet, looking down on the place called Angel Valley. They say angels can be witnessed there—felt at the altars, seen in the clouds. That hazy day I looked up to see a white band arching across the sky, like a rainbow, but colorless. Or maybe all the colors, unified. What I saw looked more like a dragon. And then, crossing in front of it, a raven. A real one.

Looking down into the valley I saw the green ribbon of Oak Creek, pine cottages with green painted roofs, a few scattered tents, a stone labyrinth, stone circle altars. The white head and tail of a bald eagle soaring below me. And farther off, some bushy-tailed animal slinking near the blue dot of my own tent. Fox? Weasel? Perspective can be confusing. Some warm-blooded furred life, anyway.

I could hear power—a ringing in my ears like a TV on in the next room. Except I was outside, no power lines in sight. Crickets, maybe, or far-off cicadas. Some would suggest it was vortex energy. I'd be just as content with cicadas. Still energy buzzing, but energy you can see, and touch. Like me.

I listened, and watched. Felt and wondered and breathed. On the earth and yet apart from it. In my body and of my mind.

And then, I happened to look over at a curved shape in a juniper tree and recognized a tiny cup nest hanging from a fork in the twigs. There atop it was a bejeweled hummingbird. At that moment the branch shifted in the wind and the sun caught the iridescent green of her back, sending out a green flash more brilliant and more stunning than the one seen in the perfect light of an open horizon over the Pacific. A flash that blinded me for a brief second. It was as if the world itself reached out for me, signaled me, marked *me*. I think I'm speaking metaphorically. But maybe not.

Because *I Am*, I could recognize that *You Are*, too. You, hummingbird, soon to be a mother. And you, mammal near my tent, sniffing out lunch. You cicadas, chanting about the heat. Even you, river, polishing stones. I was not alone, was never alone. Each other, its own being, its own voice, its own god. I was small again, an infinitesimal fragment of a whole. Was that so terrible?

It wasn't terrible at all.

I was awed to elation. Jubilant to bursting. Ecstatic! My purest, most aware self in intimate relationship with this beautiful, mysterious, magnificent world. If pressed, I might even call it a religious experience. Maybe. I do know that it's the kind of thing that only happens when the *I* that is my inner voice is perfectly, consciously aware of my body and all its senses, so that I am perfectly, wholly present in the world outside, and that it's better than any drug.

Side Effects

Important: How to Use This Information

This is a summary and does NOT have all possible information about this temperament. This information does not assure that this temperament is safe, effective, or appropriate for you. This information is not individual medical advice and does not substitute for the advice of your health care professional. Ask your doctor or pharmacist for complete information about this temperament and your specific health needs.

HIGHLY SENSITIVE PERSON
(HI-lee SEN-si-tiv PUR-sun) (HSP)
Common Brand Names: Thin-skinned; Empath; Sponge

Storage:
Do not expose to gray skies and rain for extended periods. Do not expose to direct sunlight for extended periods. Avoid high winds and dryness. Avoid high heat and humidity. Keep cool, but don't freeze.

Precautions and Contraindications:

Alcohol, sugar, caffeine, carbohydrates, cheese, chocolate, or lack thereof may change how this temperament works or increase your risk for side effects. Hormonal cycles will interact with this temperament. Avoid crowds. Avoid bright lights. Avoid loud noises such as barking dogs, raised voices, crying babies, sirens, fireworks, and gunfire; thunderstorms are generally safe. Do not under any circumstances work in retail. Limit exposure to the news. Caution is advised around politics. Caution is advised around family members. Caution is advised around the full moon.

Side Effects:

+ You may experience obsessive thinking, resembling a blaring out-of-tune radio broadcast in your head that you can't turn off. This can cause edginess and sleeplessness, which will in turn exacerbate other side effects. See below.

+ Thin skin, figurative: your tendency to soak up pain, anger, and fear in your environment may lead to jumpiness, teeth clenching, aversion to eye contact, shrinking/hiding from conflict – i.e. turtling– and/or complete withdrawal from humanity.

- Thin skin, literal: due to your lack of an adequate protective layer, you will physically react to anything and everything that touches you. You will therefore be prone to infuriatingly itchy rashes anywhere on the body. Your skin may crawl and when you inevitably scratch until it bleeds, it will form topographies of red scabby mounds and itch even more. For example, if your country were to elect a misogynistic, xenophobic, homophobic white supremacist who further diminishes your faith in humanity, inauguration day could result in full-body hives that will take two months to go away despite an anti-inflammatory diet, anti-oxidants, EFAs, Benadryl, Cortisone, Prednisone, homeopathic pills and multiple anti-itch ointments you ingest/absorb/smear on, and you could find yourself at 2 a.m. scrubbing blood off the white sheets you've just discovered you unknowingly splatter-painted like a murder scene while scratching in your sleep. For example.

- Unexpected and inappropriate crying may occur.

- Unexpected and inappropriate laughing may occur.

- In extreme cases, angry outbursts reminiscent of childhood tantrums are possible. Remove sharp objects from the immediate vicinity, including but not limited to scissors, knives, shards of glass, and razor blades.

+ Jittery restlessness may occasionally lead to excessive productivity, wherein you may plan, cook, and partition all your lunches for the coming week; bake banana bread, dust behind and under the furniture, polish the silver candlesticks, dust the houseplants, seamseal the tent, waterproof the boots, take the car in for servicing, launder all the blankets, paint your nails and then paint them again a different color, pluck your eyebrows, cut your hair, pay the bills, write actual letters, and buy more books which you won't be able to read right now because you couldn't possibly sit still that long.

+ Check with your doctor if you feel the urge to run away, off into the mountains where you would strip naked and keep running until you can't run anymore then stop, lie down, look up at the stars and feel the wind go through you like the trees until you cannot feel the cold anymore.

+ Check with your doctor if you feel the urge to go to the river and wade in with the salmon, to splash, thrash, and fight against the current with them until all the fight is gone from you and you can crawl depleted up onto a grassy knoll under a cedar to breathe in the sunshine, dazing in and out of dreams. Dry leaves rustling, river rushing, salmon slapping in the shallows.

+ Check with your doctor if you feel like a forest creature, creeping, slinking, stalking, rocking on your haunches, listening, sniffing, seeing everything, devouring food for the taste of it, craving sex and maybe also blood, something to sink your teeth into and hold on.

Long-term Use

Warning! Once you habituate to this temperament, you may experience any or all of the following:

+ Heightened enjoyment of sensual pleasures such as the luscious taste of your favorite foods on your tongue or the electric touch of a lover.

+ A tendency to be deeply moved by beauty in all its forms, but especially music, visual art, and the colors, sounds, and complexities of the natural world. Reactions may include spontaneous heart-clutching, excessive grinning, and/or happy tears.

+ Gentleness with others, the sort of sensitivity and delicate kindness you would like to be shown. Though you won't always succeed, kindness should improve with age because you will have learned time and again how a harsh word or cold look is like a swift kick in the face of your inner velvet-nosed wagging puppy, and you never ever want to cause that kind of harm to anyone else, ever.

+ If you are willing to be vulnerable, you have the capacity to connect with others genuinely, deeply, and passionately. Know your limits; you may not be able to withstand romantic love.

+ In the calms between storms when everything and everyone around you seems content, when your own body is not itchy or in pain and your mind has paused from obsessing, you will know a Zen-like blissed-out peace bordering on enlightenment, and at those times you can sit still for hours smiling in the sun or the rain listening to the birds and watching the trees in the wind just enjoying being alive.

+ Because your restlessness and discomfort will keep you continually seeking out more fitting, more nourishing, more evolving situations and experiences, you will be immune to a major midlife crisis.

+ Because you are constantly examining your life, you have few regrets and know that you are living fully.

+ As a highly sensitive individual, you will learn and remember your place in the world. You will understand that you are just one animal, one life on an earth full of other lives, animate and inanimate. You will understand what a scientific impossibility and a blessing and a miracle it is that you are here in the first place, and you will regularly be overcome with tearful gratitude that this temperament lets you experience every magical excruciating wonder-full confusing bit of it in every ounce of your being. And you wouldn't have it any other way.

This is not a complete list of possible side effects. This temperament will affect each individual differently. Contact your doctor or pharmacist for further information.
Information last revised December 2020

PART II: ECOLOGY

Animal & Earth

Outside This Skin

I was raised by two shrinks. That's what I used to boast as a kid trying to impress my friends. I still occasionally say it as an adult. I'm so used to saying it that I sometimes forget that it's not actually true.

My mother was a nurse in my early childhood and became a mental health counselor in my early adolescence; she wasn't technically a Ph.D. "shrink" until I was out of her house. My stepfather the psychologist moved in when I was nine, and though in the end he logged more in-house fatherhood years than my biological father, I'm not sure I would say he raised me. But it sounded cool and somewhat rebellious to say I was raised by two shrinks. For a kid who was neither cool nor rebellious, the shrink card was one of the few I held.

Other kids would squint their eyes and scrutinize me like a peculiar insect, and say things like: *Wow, they must analyze you all the time.*

Yes, I would nod, putting on my pensive face, *It's awful.*

Which isn't true either, or if it was, I wouldn't have noticed. I was too busy analyzing myself.

A psychological parental milieu concurrent with the narcissism of adolescence may have magnified the effect, but it started long before both. I had always felt like a fraud, as if someone had squeezed me into a human suit and left me here without instructions, and that this was blatantly obvious to everyone else. How everyone else always seemed to know how to act around each other was baffling.

On the school bus to first grade when a barrage of strange faces aimed at me, I thought that the best way to make friends would be to smile. Day after day when I wasn't sure what to say or do, I just smiled. But when the big kids started calling me Smiley it didn't feel like making friends, it felt like the ache in my stomach when my parents fought. So I stopped smiling.

On the school bus to second grade my new friend Sally told me *Close your mouth. You look retarded.* I hadn't realized it had been open. I looked over at her, mouth closed and hands folded in her lap. Slick chestnut ponytail in order. I attempted to smooth my straw-colored snarls. I was learning that I had to pay attention to my body, to keep it reined in, behaving so that it didn't draw attention to itself. I shut my mouth.

By high school I thought I had it figured out. When to smile and when to keep my eyes down. What to say and how to behave to play the part of daughter, student, teenager, human. Most of the time I was pretty good at it. You know, raised by two shrinks. I was supposed to have my shit together.

Except, like many (most?) teenagers, I didn't. Chalk it up to adolescent hormones, the situational stresses of high school, or another impending parental divorce. Or maybe it was the building tension of spending so much time worrying about how to be normal and feeling like a fake. For whatever reason,

I started crying all the time. I cried when my mother and stepfather woke me up fighting, and when I couldn't sleep because I was worried they would start fighting. When I stubbed my toe, set off the deafening house alarm, or when my little sister jumped out and scared me, I cried. When an infant wailed or a dog barked or I was just tired, I sobbed. Red-faced and puffy-eyed, no amount of cold water could erase it, and no matter how hard I slapped my face or yelled at my reflection in the mirror the tears kept running, burning crimson tracks down my cheeks. Betrayed by my own body.

The betrayal caused something else, something different simmering in that tight place in my stomach. Something called rage that demanded action. Like a wolverine trapped inside trying to claw its way out. I pierced my ears—pushed pointy studs through without icing first and watched the blood run. Then pierced them again. It felt good. Calming. I was in charge of my world instead of just passively absorbing it. I could stop crying and breathe again.

There was power in that way of reining my body in, and I dabbled in the tools of my new art—cinder block walls for knuckles; knives, broken glass, and razor blades for the skin of my legs, stomach, chest, arms. Razor blades became my favorite; they cut deeply and cleanly, summoned blood quickly. I became adept at breaking the plastic casing off of disposable razors—pink shards in the trash and the blades in the drawer of my nightstand—my little secret.

Dressed in black with shaggy hair in my eyes, I sat cross-legged on my purple rug, Suzanne Vega's "Solitude Standing"[10] lamenting on my boombox. A single quick slice to the skin above my left breast would start the blood and stop the tears. Soothe the savage beast, for a little while.

Even then I recognized the irony, the after-school special material at work in the shrinks' house. But I was in control of my own body again and that was all that mattered. Nobody needed to know about it; in public, I could go back to behaving the way I thought I was supposed to.

Until one day after a hectic school week, I went a little nuts with a razor blade on the back of my hand and said a cat scratched me, but I wasn't fooling anyone. My mother confronted me and made me see a shrink. Or technically, a counselor, who had an office across the street from my school. She was a gentle woman with curly brown hair, puppy dog eyes, and a voice like maple syrup. Her office was full of stuffed animals and she hugged me at the beginning and end of every session. It turned out she knew my mother. Cue after-school special part two.

So I went every week and I cried again and said sorry, a lot, for being abnormal. I knew talking was supposed to make it all better, and it did help a little, but I didn't have a whole lot to talk about because I knew there was no good reason to be so upset in the first place. But I promised not to cut anymore because she said I was hurting other people and that was never the point. "Do you know how concerned your parents are? How your actions make them feel?"

Of course I knew. Shrinks don't tend to have trouble voicing their feelings. "Shrink guilt" is a lot like Catholic guilt or Jewish guilt, just with less God and more jargon like narcissism, deflection, and repression.

In college, I got an internship at a boarding school for severely ADHD, high functioning autistic, and other 'abnormal' kids. Where a simple disagreement in the dining hall might lead to a ten-year-old holding a knife to another's throat. One evening in the dorms when a twelve-year-old began screaming and tearing posters off the walls, I found myself saying that there was no good reason for his behavior. When he screamed louder that yes, there was, I knew he was right. It's just the reason had less to do with the easy explanations of cause and effect and more to do with the whole big overwhelming world.

I majored in psychology, though I was quick to announce that *I don't plan to go on in it; I just think it's interesting.* Which was true, the human psyche was interesting. If I was going to live in this skin I might as well get to the bottom of the business of being human, normal or abnormal. I figured my Psych 101 book held the operating instructions. I was going to figure it all out.

I learned new labels like bipolar and borderline personality disorder and, like Psych students everywhere, secretly thought I had everything. I loved school and hated parties, which I knew weren't the normal sentiments, but it was so much work to try to be social, to be funny or cool or rebellious or something other than wallflower, and there were always too many people and the music was too loud. In private I still cried and raged and sometimes even cut, since I no longer had a shrink to answer to.

After college I worked my way through multiple jobs on multiple career paths, trying and regularly failing to find a place where I could be myself, no faking. And even though I feared I was too emotionally fragile to work with 'abnormal' kids, I was still drawn to them. They made sense in a way that the other kids never did. So I got a job working with severely autistic kids in a home therapy program. I worked daily with three little boys, trying to help them learn language and social skills, to fit in with the rest of us. You know, because I was such a prime specimen of normalcy.

Three months in, I was still uncomfortable in my role. Though I could see that in general the program was helping the boys learn to express themselves and connect with their families, I questioned whether our strict protocols were necessary. Whether it actually was a good thing to attempt to make these kids just like the rest, whether they were the ones who needed fixing.

At the end of one ordinary, trying day of training a nearly non-verbal six year old in typical human kid behaviors, all that was left on my company-dictated to-do list was to facilitate him sitting in a chair and completing a puzzle with six pieces.

Simple directions, manual dexterity, and problem-solving skills that wouldn't ruffle most two-year-olds. Once he did that, he would be free to leave our window-less closet-turned-classroom and have unscheduled time until dinner. He'd completed the puzzle before. Multiple times. Which may have been part of the problem.

"Listen to me. Sit down. Finish this puzzle, and then you're all done."

He looked sideways at me and cringed like I was a snake about to strike. Then jumped up, ran to the door, and jiggled the handle. Which was locked. He brought a bruised wrist to his mouth, bit down, and then yelled *All Done!*

"No, puzzle first," I said in my calmest, most soothing adult voice I could muster, "*then* all done."

He ran over to me, grabbed a fistful of my bruised arm flesh in his little boy fingers and pinched, hard. *ALL DONE!!*

I removed my arm from his grip, tapped the empty chair, and then the puzzle on the table and said, "No. Puzzle." But my voice was getting shaky.

He started to wail, jumping, flapping, slapping at himself. And then the tears came. For both of us. The six-year-old screaming and rocking on the floor and the twenty-five-year-old crying and rocking in the chair, both trapped and helpless.

And I gave up. Not on him, but myself.

That was the beginning of the end. The end of engaging with making other people normal, and the end of trying to fit in myself.

I started saying No.

When people invited me to parties, I said No. When friends wanted to set me up on dates saying I should be in a relationship, I said No. After spending three days cooped up with my family trying to play the part of doting daughter, when my mother saw me crying and suggested I might be Depressed, I could confidently say No.

During a gynecological exam under blinding buzzing fluorescent lights with my legs in stirrups and a cold stranger's hand inside me, when I started feeling like a trapped animal and began shaking and crying uncontrollably and the doctor tried to prescribe anti-depressants, I said No.

I was finally learning that crying doesn't necessarily mean sadness. That for me, it rarely does.

I stayed home a lot, nose in a book. Mostly, books about exploring the world outside human culture, the natural world. I discovered nature writing.

And I went out alone, walking, hiking, swimming, birding, or just sitting in the woods. Butt in the dirt, back against a tree, birds going about their business around me, I would slowly disappear until there was no me and no such thing as normal. I could smile or stare open-mouthed or rock or whimper and none of it mattered.

And you know what? I stopped crying all the time. Stopped raging. Alone on a forest trail where I didn't need to squint or plug my ears or manage my body or say the right thing, I was happy. Not just comfortably content, but so euphorically gleeful that I might giggle like a baby. No good reason.

The more time I spent by myself outside, the more psychology seemed like a silly construct designed by a silly species. A discipline as small-minded and self-absorbed as the teenager (okay, adult) that I was (okay, am). Outside was a living world where the study of the psyche didn't apply. A world that had been going on a long time before we came on the scene with our personality disorders and our coping mechanisms. Outside a honeybee danced an earth story to her sisters, encoding the exact location of a flower. Outside a jay mimicked a redtailed hawk two minutes ahead of the hawk's arrival. Outside a cottonwood tree stretched roots through dry soil toward a water seep in the cedar grove. Outside, everything seemed to fit with everything else, distinct and yet connected.

I used my experience working with kids to get a job in environmental education, then held a variety of seasonal jobs in wildlife conservation, which culminated in graduate school in field ecology. The more I learned, the more I felt connected to, rather than separate from my world. I wasn't the center of it anymore, didn't matter much at all. Which was comforting. Calming. Eco– comes from the Greek oikos, meaning house. The earth as one big house where we all live. Unlike Dorothy, I had to step out of my own psyche to find my home.

One day I was chatting with a coworker about past lives, entertaining the possibilities, and she said, "Sometimes I think I haven't been a woman for a while, you know?" Meaning that she didn't feel particularly adept at womanhood, so maybe she'd been a man in recent lives. I think she expected agreement due to my self-cropped hair, baggy clothes, and linebacker physique.

Without thinking I answered, "Actually, I think I haven't been human for a while. Or ever."

It was an intriguing thought. Maybe I was so challenged by living in this skin because I'd never done it before. I was used to being a different kind of animal, metaphysically speaking. It might explain my reaction when one of my summer campers bragged that he'd kicked a skunk and I wanted more than anything to kick that child. People chasing peacocks at the zoo to pull out their tail feathers or shooting snakes just because they dislike them spark the same reaction. I never feel more alienated from my own species than the times they (we?) are brazenly cruel to other animals. Those who stomp on spiders are as foreign and horrifying to me as spiders probably are to them. Which isn't to say that I'm some big compassionate softie. I did want to kick that kid. Pull the hair of the peacock chasers, shoot the snake killers, and stomp on the spider stompers. I know, bad human. Which is exactly my point.

But there I go looking for explanations again. I might as well order up the latest DSM, whatever number we're on.

Times like those I need to back away, Just Say No for a while, wander alone in the wilds until I forget psychology and remember ecology.

And then, once I do, I need to consider saying Yes.

Like that spring morning a few years back when I went on a silent nature walk with a group of adults. We were asked not to speak at all, but encouraged to interact with each other and the natural world. In the spearmint green of a riverside cedar grove in central Washington I shed the pressure to conform or entertain. Instead of wondering what to say, I spoke with my eyes and my hands. Found them much better at the task. We all looked at one another, nodded often, pointed at everything. The perfect fiddlehead of a new fern, the thorns on a devil's club leaf. The jubilant song of a pacific wren. Our eyes said how beautiful! Our eyes said how awesome! Our eyes said aren't we lucky to be here, together, away from everything stressful and painful and overwhelming back there? Or I was pretty sure that's what we were saying. Or maybe we were living in a place beyond the simple explanations of cause and effect. I do know that instead of the forced smile I often don for *the public*, I found myself grinning with unrestrained euphoric glee. And that time, faces like my own grinned back at me. I have rarely felt so calm, so grounded, so safe.

Or the summer afternoon I supervised a small group of twelve-year-olds who'd chosen to spend an hour at a lakeside New Hampshire nature center, and we discovered dozens of new adult dragonflies hanging on the side of the building, kaleidoscopic wings drying in the sun. We lay on our bellies in the grass and watched, quietly, still, so as not to scare them. Staring at the new lives unfurling before me, I didn't disappear as I would have if I'd been alone. I was still aware of myself and of the others around me. But it was a good kind of awareness, a warm fuzzy kind of togetherness, of sharing something special. My mouth was open the whole time, and catching the sparkling eyes of my companions, I discovered theirs were too.

Or the winter evening in North Cascades National Park, when a group of high school kids followed me on a snowy trail glowing in moonlight. How I glanced back to find they'd all adopted my habit of patting the giant grandmother firs and cedars and saying *thank you* as we passed. I hadn't known they'd noticed me doing it, but didn't care what they thought. They were teenagers; I assumed they thought I was a nerd, and I was okay with that. But I saw them, all nine of them, some grinning sheepishly, some serious. Pat pat. *Thank you, tree.*

Once I climbed out of my own mind and found my home on earth, I started connecting with other humans, for real. Without acting, without pretending, without even trying.

I find them in the forest, but also in the music I listen to, the books I read. Other humans who make me look out from my insular world and say *Yes!* In an essay by musician and author Kristin Hersh, I discovered these words: "On fire, underwater, wherever you are, your people are waiting for you to care. Their investment floats you back up to the surface. Where, of course, you can't help but paddle around a little and glance over at the shore. And there's always something there to hold your gaze."[11]

My people. I used to think I didn't have people, but perhaps I do. Perhaps we all do. They are the ones who, in their presence, make us comfortable in our own skins, who make us okay with being human. I spent the day with some of them recently. Eleven people between the ages of sixteen and seventy-six, a couple old friends but mostly strangers, all piled in a van at 6:30 one clear May morning for a daylong birding road trip. Driving through river gorges, across sagebrush desert, and up and over a mountain we were trying to count as many bird species as we could before the sun swung to the west. Each time out of the van we'd get right to listening, peering through binoculars, whispering questions, and exclaiming at each new discovery. Witnessing the white pelican, wings shining silver in the desert sun against the cobalt sky, the badger kits jousting outside their burrow in a rancher's field, the western kingbird reigning over his nest in a riverside cottonwood tree, or a rare (to us) Say's phoebe flycatching from decorative antlers hung on a saloon door, we all joined in the delighted glee of connecting with our world and each other. We laughed together at the canyon wren's swirling descending song, and squatted together to peer at delicate calypso orchids blooming fuchsia in a montane forest. I barely spoke two words to some of them, didn't exchange small talk about who we were or what we did outside of that day, because it didn't matter. That day, we were family. All day long I thought, *I don't want this to end. Can't we do this again tomorrow?* That, I think, is what it feels like to find your people.

The highlight of my day was a roadside lunch stop at the edge of a ponderosa grove. We scattered a little in our preferences for sun or shade, company or solitude, wandering off separately or clumping up in easy conversation or silence. A horse walked up from an adjacent pasture and stood standing at the corner of her fence, watching us. I went to her immediately. After letting her sniff the back of my hand, I nuzzled the whiskers of her chin. She sighed, letting her head droop heavy into my hand. I leaned into her with my head, then started scratching her neck under her mane. The dust coming off her suggested she hadn't been brushed for a while and it clouded the air with sweet horsey perfume. She leaned her head closer and we stood together, cheek to cheek. I alternated scratching her neck and letting her nibble my fingers with her lips, gently with closed teeth.

I was in love. I don't mean that abstract psychobabble word but the real-life, physiological response. My heart pounded, my face flushed, and I felt as blissfully content as I ever have in the presence of my deepest human loves. I wanted nothing more than to be near that horse, and I knew—with my body, not my brain—she felt the same.

Maybe, in a past life I was a wild horse, wandering those sagebrush hills under vanilla-scented ponderosa pines. On the other hand, maybe that horse used to be human. Or maybe, when it comes down to it, there isn't as big a difference as we think. Aren't we all just stardust, dressed in different skins? Human suit, fur suit, scaly suit or feathered, don't we have so much more in common?

And yet, I do think our silly species is special. The fact that we can look out from our own psyches and wonder, question, even analyze the world outside ourselves is a gift and a challenge. To look out and only see our own kind is just another form of narcissism. What a blessing to look out and see a dusty horse in a ponderosa grove and know that there, too, stands my people.

TO REMAIN SILENT

AWKWARD

Silence? Rarely. Speech? Almost always.

BABY BIRD

Remain silent until Mom or Dad returns. Only then might you open your mouth wider than your head and cheep, chatter, chirp, or squawk to ensure you get some of that tasty worm. The rest of the time, you best hunker down and shut your beak, or you will be somebody else's lunch.

CYBERSPACE

A modern human can chat all day without ever uttering a word. *Tap tap tap* on the keyboard; *tick tick tick* on the smartphone. Swipe and send. You can meet in cyberspace, flirt, date, have cybersex, and break up without making a sound. Communication devices advance, shrink, and move ever closer to our bodies, from our desks to our laps to our hands to our wrists… soon we may be uploading messages directly into each other's minds.

DUMB

Of Germanic origin, a word originally meaning mute—temporarily or permanently lacking the ability to speak. According to the Oxford Dictionary, "In Old English dumb ... could apply to both humans and animals." Only in the middle ages did the word begin to connote unintelligent or stupid.

EXPOSED

I worked for a time at a hot springs retreat center that offered clothing-optional bathing pools. Few people wore anything while soaking. My first week there, January in the Oregon Cascades, I met several of my new coworkers while we were all naked, in broad daylight, often not even in the cover of the soaking tubs. I shook hands while tiptoeing on icy gravel toward the steaming water or back to my clothes on the wooden bench, arms and legs in gooseflesh, nipples at attention in the frosty sunshine. There's no hiding then. No way to not be yourself. When you're naked, small talk seems particularly absurd. Then again, some of us feel like that all the time.

FAITH

Ever since our ancestors sat gazing into their fires silently contemplating the Big Mystery, there have been those who connect most deeply with that something bigger than ourselves through silence.

Thomas Merton was a member of the Trappist Order of monks in the early 1900s. Though the Trappists don't take a strict vow of silence, they traditionally do not speak and use sign language to communicate. In his memoir *The Seven Storey Mountain*, this silent monk wrote 462 pages on his journey to silence. Across time, space, and belief systems Merton's written words helped me understand one version of Christianity better than any pontificating preacher ever had. Beyond the dogma, beyond the rules of asceticism, here was a striving, struggling man seeking a life of substance, of deeper meaning than he found in the everyday human world. His choice to become a monk was a choice to live in a way that felt more real, to him. "Contemplation means rest, suspension of activity, withdrawal into the mysterious interior solitude in which the soul is absorbed in the immense and fruitful silence of God..."[12]

Are we so different? Not that I'm going to run out and join a nunnery anytime soon. At least I don't think so.

GATHER YOUR THOUGHTS

My thoughts are like timid rabbits. The real ones, the ones that matter, they only seem to come around when it's silent. When I'm silent, and when the world around me is silent. No speaking, no music, no traffic noise, no refrigerator hum. Maybe a little birdsong or river gurgling or wind in the trees, because those are just different versions of silence. When it's silent like that, the rabbits come out. And like Snow White, I can gather them to me where they whisper the most wonderful things.

Until the thumping bass notes from a car revving by or the bang of the neighbor boys shooting bb's or even the drone of human commerce in an open-plan office and they all scatter, willy nilly, some never to be seen again.

HAWK

Songbirds are the messengers of the forest. Attending to their alarm calls can inform you a predator is near. More telling than insistent chips cheeps or shrieks of an alarming bird is a sudden, oppressive silence. One minute, multiple species are singing. The next, a few alarming. Then, nothing.

Look up. Or down. Something dangerous is nearby, something too scary even to risk the announcement. Something is out there, right here, actively hunting, and the songbirds know it. Their silence says it all.

INTROVERT

If you prefer the role of silent observer, you are probably an introvert. In *Quiet, The Power of Introverts in a World That Can't Stop Talking*, Susan Cain presents modern research and extensive anecdotes to make any introvert nod so frequently and passionately (though silently) as to get whiplash. Cain explains that "participation places a very different set of demands on the brain than observing does. It requires a kind of mental multitasking: the ability to process a lot of short-term information at once without becoming distracted or overly stressed. This is just the sort of brain functioning that extroverts tend to be well suited for. … So when introverts assume the observer role, as when they write novels, or contemplate unified field theory— or fall quiet at dinner parties—they're not demonstrating a failure of will or a lack of energy. They're simply doing what they're constitutionally suited for." [13]

JANUARY

January is the quietest month in the northern hemisphere, just after we've tilted fully away from the sunshine, toward the darkness, before we can feel any movement the other direction. The farther from the equator, the deeper the winter quiet.

In January, there's nowhere quieter than a snowbound mountain. Most of the wildlife have gone away, gone to sleep, or are otherwise hunkered down, saving their energy. In January, if you happen to find yourself on a snowbound mountain, say in the North Cascades of Washington, you might find yourself using the cliché, *dead silent*. It's as if the whole world holds her breath, afraid even to exhale. The silence is loud. Deafening, even, a void ringing in your ears. January's silence is oppressive. And yet, much of the rest of the year you'd give anything to escape there.

KATYDID

The summer soundscape of my Connecticut youth was dominated by long-antennaed nocturnal "bush crickets," rarely seen but easily heard. Syncopated onomatopoeic chanting emanated from forewings rubbed together. The hotter the night, the faster the tempo. More Katies doing their thing. *Katy did; Katy didn't. Katy Katy did did didn't.* The cooler the night, the fewer and slower the Katies.

Kaytey… did.

Kay…tey…did…n't.

Until fall, when Katy refrains from arguing until the heat returns the following summer.

LIBRARIES

Have you been to a library lately? The libraries I've visited are not the silent escapes they used to be, they are bustling community centers. Meet-up locations. Internet cafes. Cell phones beep and tone. Nobody shushes anyone anymore. Where can one go, in the presence of other people, where quiet is expected?

MIRANDA

You have the right to remain silent. Anything you say can and will be used against you.

NATURALISTS

When a lofty shadow drifted in front of the sun three of us rose from our haunches to seek its source. Three pairs of eyes squinted toward the brightest light to find the dark shape while the rest remained squatting among diminutive prairie flowers. We spied a dark head, broad wings pale enough that the sunlight illuminated individual feathers, and a cinnamon tail fanned wide against the cobalt sky. It circled, higher, lifting silently to the heavens. While six people squatted, still listening to the hike leader talk about the rare white delphinium, we three stood tall, facing the sun and the red-tailed hawk. We smiled at the hawk, and we smiled at each other. No words. Three strangers connected in the place beyond words.

We three then knew to seek each others' eyes the next time a raptor flew over, a lazuli bunting sang, or a cinnabar moth scared up from a tansy flower. Each time, our smiles grew wider, the sorts of smiles that lit up our whole faces and made our hearts thump a little faster. We recognized something in each other that said "a plant walk is never just a plant walk," and something that said "this is my deepest passion too" and "hey, you are like me." But of course, we wouldn't say those things out loud.

OR FOREVER HOLD YOUR PEACE

Silence = Peace. Therefore, Speaking up =

PREGNANT PAUSE

A silence full of the promise of something important; the anticipation of what is to follow.

QUAKER

In major religions the Word of God (Yahweh, Allah, etc.) is usually spoken aloud by a preacher (minister, rabbi, imam, etc.) Unless you're a Quaker, where a generally leaderless group of "Friends" meets to sit for an hour together in silence. In a recent episode of the online video series, "QuakerSpeak," author and Quaker Ben Pink Dandelion explains, "…we've found over the centuries that we have a very strong sense of presence that comes through absence. We can say that absence leads to a sense of presence."[14]

RABBITS

Rabbits have vocal cords like most mammals, but they rarely use them. They communicate through complex body language. An erect tail is a sign of aggression. A jump straight up with a half-twist in midair is the equivalent of kicking up your heels, jumping for joy. The faster the nose wiggling, the more attentive and alert (though not alarmed). Slow wiggling means calm and peaceful. Leg thumping is a warning. The one instance a rabbit typically breaks its vow of silence is near death, which for prey animals is rarely old age. In sheer terror or tremendous pain, rabbits scream.

SEEN AND NOT HEARD

When I was a park ranger I led a preschool program called "Story & Stroll." Read a nature story, then lead a related stroll. For a high-strung anxious educator hyperconcerned with teaching perfectly and keeping everyone happy, preschoolers were sure to whip me into a frenzied frazzle every time. Except once.

The book had something to do with being quiet, so I attempted to lead a quiet walk. With preschoolers. To give the kids a way to communicate, I taught the ASL signs for tree, bird, and bug. Three words. A group of twelve two to four-year-olds, their parents and I walked the path into the forest and found that those three words were enough. We looked into each other's eyes, we pointed, we tapped shoulders, we jumped up and down and clapped our hands and we saw so many trees, birds, and bugs that day. Maybe we giggled a little bit, and maybe we squealed once or twice before we shushed ourselves, and probably one or two tantrumed at some point, but the rest of the time, we were perfectly quiet. And in that silence I could suddenly and maybe for the first time recognize the light in their eyes, the simultaneous innocence and wisdom and above all the hope, and I wanted more than anything to gather them all up and hold on to them, hold on to this, to freeze us there forever.

And then we got back to the nature center and commenced gabbing and screeching and whining and proclaiming and I forgot.

THANKSGIVING

My mother and her new husband lay head to toe on the couch like teenagers. My father tucked in to his easy chair, feet up on his hassock. My sister and her five-year-old snuggled on the rug, and I sat by the window, binoculars on my lap. All of us wore pajamas and blankets, nuzzled pillows, and sipped ginger ale or peppermint tea. The television hummed a football game or maybe it was the latest overplayed holiday matinee, barely audible, and nobody said anything. For hours.

This was the year of the thanksgiving plague, where one by one we'd each succumbed to the nastiest of combination intestinal stomach bugs. On the day after turkey day when the last one of us went down, we tossed the leftovers in the trash and admitted defeat. There would be no rousing games of Yahtzee, no wintry walks through the frozen Montana hills, no Lego houses with my niece, and minimal progress on the newly opened puzzle. There would also be no pestering, no bickering, no passive-aggressive guilt trips, no placation, no lectures, no spats, and no demands.

Mom sighed. Becca whimpered. Dad ran to one of two bathrooms, both of which hadn't seen so much action in the two years he'd lived there. I watched a white-breasted nuthatch scold a fox squirrel at the feeder above a family of wild turkeys scratching in gray snow.

This was my favorite family holiday, ever. Sure, my insides felt like they were trying to escape from both ends at the same time, and I mourned the turkey sandwich I wouldn't eat. But my family was... calm. Quiet. Gentle with each other. Not asking anything of each other, or more to the point, me. I was free to sit, and think. Not be entertainer or entertained. Not dwell on bad memories or fixate on underlying tensions. Just be with my family, my sweet loving puking sick silent family. I may never have loved them more.

UNLESS SPOKEN TO

There are those of us who have rarely heard this advice, even as children. What would we possibly say if someone else hadn't started the conversation? Only in my adulthood did I learn that to be a good friend or just a polite person, I was supposed to ask others about themselves, not wait for them to open up on their own. Ask follow-up questions, continue to engage. Other people like that, it seems. Still, it rarely comes naturally. I say what I think I'm supposed to say, what will sound good, what I think they want to hear. I want to be myself, to make myself understood, to connect with other people, but mostly it feels like I'm trying and failing at a foreign language. Mostly I don't feel like me.

Speech defines, it extrapolates and explains, and in doing so it limits. It isn't enough, never enough. To define is to restrict, preclude other possibilities. What if I get it wrong? How do we ever get it right?

It's not that I don't have the words. There are always words, usually swirling in my head. Remembered ones, from the day past, and imagined ones, from the day to come. Instant replay on skip. Planned scenarios on repeat. The exercise of a busy mind trying to make sense, debrief, and prepare. The right ones are there, I am sure. But getting the right ones to come forward at the right time is beyond me. Did I say that? Why did I say that? That isn't what I meant at all.

VOICELESS

I used to wish I didn't speak, that I couldn't. Then I could remain in my head where it may be loud and crowded, but at least I would feel like myself. I could connect with people without pretending, without donning someone else's clothing.

Until one winter after a long bout of bronchitis confounded with the grief of mourning the end of a relationship, I lost my voice. It stayed lost long after the rest of my body was healthy. For five weeks I could only whisper. Knowing that it was probably all in my head didn't help; I physically could not make a sound. I would face the mirror and try to scream, but couldn't. Air whistled through my throat. Just air. What I thought should be a comfort was a prison. What if it never came back?

Thirty-five days of silence.

On day thirty-six, I hummed. Then I sang. I groaned and laughed and squealed and wailed just because I could. I will never wish myself silent again.

We are noisy animals. We arrive screaming and we gurgle and babble our way into the world of words but we keep up the other sounds too, clicking, snorting, whistling, guffawing, and grunting our way through the world, often whether we are actively communicating with others or not.

WRITING

Writing is the only way I've found to let the words out in a way that feels authentic to me. I can speak my peace and still remain silent.

XY

Male birds sing to attract mates and maintain territory. But song learning and refining is energetically expensive, and mainly needed in spring. In late summer males do not just choose to be silent to save energy; their brains shrink. Individual neurons lose mass, requiring less fuel and taking up less weight that would be costly in migration and predator evasion. Use it or lose it? Waste not want not.

Late August can be as quiet as January. Not dead silent, just, quiet. Calm. The most peaceful month of all.

YAWP

I too am not a bit tamed, I too am untranslatable,
I sound my barbaric yawp over the roofs of the world.[15]
–Walt Whitman

All of us, even the silent ones, especially the silent ones, occasionally, even if only in private, need to open wide and yell, scream, yawp. For none of us is fully tamed or ever wholly translatable.

ZEITGEIST

We live in a noisy time. Even if you yourself remain silent, you will still likely be immersed in noise. These days silence is not a passive experience but an active pursuit. You have to seek it out. And when you find it, in all the big and little ways you find it, you'll give it your full attention.

Free Hands

I tasted blood. Must have been picking at my lips again. Scraping that bump in the middle of my top lip as if to smooth a seam, or pulling away any chapped strips. Which leaves more uneven surfaces to mess with, more topography for my fingers to find and excavate when I'm not paying attention. I looked down to see red on the tips of my index finger and thumb. Guilty.

Raccoons are mammals in the Carnivora order. You may know them as the bandits who raid your trash cans or cat food dishes left outside, who drive your dogs crazy from just beyond reach in trees or under porches, who have learned to open latches and turn doorknobs and are bold enough to invite themselves into your home for a midnight snack. As with other adaptable, omnivorous, wily scavengers like coyotes, crows, rats, and humans, their populations are on the rise throughout North America and as introduced invasive species in Europe and Asia.

I never wanted to put my hands in those black boxes at Halloween parties labeled worms or eyeballs or brains, because even though I knew it was just cold spaghetti or wet grapes or molded Jello, it gave me the willies anyway. We learn young that cold and slimy is icky.

We had black boxes at the nature center where I worked in my twenties, but they held drier mysteries, wild nature mysteries like a shelf mushroom, pine cone, scrap of deer hide, or deer antler. Kids didn't want to put their hands in there either. Darkness is icky too.

The ancestors of modern raccoons evolved around riverbanks and lakes in South American tropics but migrated farther north about 4 million years ago, settling in similar regions in more temperate climates. Until European invasions they were mainly found in the southeastern United States, rarely far from water.

Raccoons will eat worms, yellow jackets, baby birds and eggs, small mammals, fruit, nuts, frogs, insects, fish, human food, and trash, but they especially love crayfish. They are experts at plunging their hands into murky waters and coming up with their shrimpy little snacks.

We had a snake at the nature center too, a beautiful four-foot ball python named Isis who I would take out from under her heat lamp to drape around my shoulders and encourage the kids to come touch her. They usually expected her to be slimy, but she wasn't. Snake and other reptile skin is a lot drier and smoother than ours, I would explain. Isis could move across the ground without picking anything up, whereas we could move our hands along the same area of earth and come up with dirty hands. Technically, that makes us slimier.

Raccoon tracks, especially from their front feet, look a lot like tiny human handprints. They have five fingers and five toes, and similar to humans and bears, raccoons place their entire footpads, or heels, flat on the ground when walking. As opposed to dogs and cats who walk on their toes. Unlike bears, raccoons have long, slender fingers. Their thumbs aren't technically opposable but that doesn't seem to stop them; raccoons have dexterity to rival most primates. They can climb, grasp, pick up and hold, turn, dig, and probe. If you could teach them to shake, they'd put your dog to shame.

For two years in massage school and five years at work, my hands learned the human body from head to toe. They felt the discreet shapes of muscles, learned to feel tension and the many ways to soothe it away. Kneading, digging, shaking, knuckling, squeezing, rocking, drumming, or sometimes, simply holding, my hands seemed to know exactly what to do. My hands were good at their work. My hands could have done that work for many more years.

The rest of me? The brain to run a business. The voice to say the right words, to suggest solutions, calm anger, soothe grief, even chat about the weather, that didn't come naturally. My hands knew nothing of bedside manner.

I moved on to other jobs, massaged friends now and then until I sold my massage table. I might give an absent-minded shoulder rub here and there, but now I mostly catch myself kneading my own neck. Knuckling up the opposite arm. Wringing my hands.

If I had to choose, I might say the baby raccoons were my favorite animals I worked with during a wildlife rehabilitation internship. As soon as you walked in the clinic door they'd coo and cry, not the nerve-frazzling screams of human babies but the heart-melting whimpers of puppies. Bottle in hand, I would walk into the orphans' closet-sized cage, sit crosslegged on the floor and allow the kits to come to me. Cool little hands padded along my legs, reached up for the bottle.

They were fussy little munchkins, hungry as they were. I couldn't just stick the bottle in a mouth and be done with it. I had to grip the bottle and fuzzy face with one hand, and scratch a back with the other hand. Otherwise, they never calmed and milk went everywhere. When I clamped on and scratched though, the little kit would release throaty purring sighs and gulp the milk right down. One hand on the bottle and the other grasping my finger.

The Latin name for the raccoon is *Procyon* (doglike) *lotor* (one who washes), for their habit of taking their food in their hands and dunking it in water before eating. If there's water around they'll use it. Even in a dish on the linoleum floor of a rehab clinic. Even if the food is already clean. You might call that obsessive-compulsive.

I pull my hair out too. Always have. Thankfully not chunks of it that would leave bald spots and grant me a label from the DSM, but one hair at a time, and only certain hairs. My fingertips smooth and sift, scratch along my scalp, pull thin strands taut in between thumb and forefinger, seeking any outliers. Coarse, curly, crimped, or knotted, I'll find it, single it out, and pluck. Then go back for more. There are always more.

Whether my hair is short or long, styled or ponytailed, or loose and wild, I seek and pluck. Usually when nobody is watching, but sometimes even when they are because I don't notice I'm doing it, I seek and pluck. I must have done it a lot as a teenager because my friends had a refrain they used on me so often it became a joke: *Stop playing with your hair; it looks fine.*

It never had anything to do with how it looked. It probably looks worse after I get through with my fussing. It's just something my hands do, independent of my intentions. Anytime one hand is idle for very long—driving, reading, pausing on my keyboard—one hand will be in my hair. That is, unless it's kneading my neck or busy with my lips.

The glabrous, or hairless areas of mammalian skin like the palms of our hands and feet are packed with nerve endings, mechanoreceptors they're called. Different types of mechanoreceptors lie in the ridged topography that give us our fingerprints, others in smooth skin. Some rest near the surface, some lodge deeper. They have important-sounding names like

Meissner's corpuscles, Pacinian corpuscles, lanceolate endings, Merkel cells, and Ruffini corpuscles. The more types of mechanoreceptors, the more sensitive the skin.

The bumpy pads of raccoon hands contain almost all of them, about four to five times the mechanoreceptors found in most mammals. In fact, the concentration and complexity of nerve endings in raccoon hands are comparable only to primates, to human hands.

Smooth plastic button of my alarm clock. Cotton clothing. Hair. Ceramic coffee mug, metal spoon. Smooth plastic computer keys. Lips. Smooth plastic cell phone screen protector. Vinyl steering wheel. Hair. Smooth plastic computer keys. Smooth plastic phone. Computer keys. Hair. Computer keys. Lips. Ceramic tea mug, fork. Cell phone. Computer keys and hair. Lips. Steering wheel and hair. Computer keys, phone. Fork. Paper pages of a book, and hair. Flannel sheets. Lips.

The common name *raccoon* comes from the Powhatan or Virginia Algonquin word *aroughcoune* or *arakun,* meaning "one who rubs or scratches with the hands." Which is a better moniker than "one who washes," because raccoons don't actually wash their food.

Raccoons evolved in the living world and developed unique tools to help them survive here. Their bodies learned how to take advantage of rich food sources in murky waters and muddy crevices. It turns out, moistening their thick fingerpads increases the sensitivity of all those corpuscles, so they could reach their hands into the blackness and find only the tastiest morsels. Raccoons learned to see with their hands.

The tips of my index finger and thumb are stained and sticky. I bring them to my nose and breathe in the sweet honey smell of cottonwood resin, the golden sap that oozes from late winter buds before they leaf out. I look around the forest floor, notice more branches down, more glistening buds ripe for the plucking, but I have enough. Enough to tuck into a jar with olive oil to sit and soak, then stir into melted beeswax and pour into tins for a rich salve. A salve to moisten and cool, soften and heal chapped lips, itchy rashes, and aching hands.

Raccoon hands refuse to forget where they came from. The muddy waters where their bodies began and long, always, to return. So, are they obsessive? Only in cages.

I feel for the knobby nodules of the licorice fern roots under a mossy maple trunk, find a section between two ferns and snap it off, leaving the foliage intact. I rub off a strand of moss and soil and place the root in my mouth, nibbling with my front teeth to savor the bittersweet tang.

I seek out the pointed holly-like leaves of an Oregon grape shrub and dig. Fir needles and cottonwood leaf litter, gritty soil, then smooth clay. Dig. I locate hairlike rootlets and course branching roots, then find the joint and snap. Pull it up into the light, rub off soil to reveal rough bark. Scratch a thumbnail under the brown to reveal the buttery yellow inner bark, the medicine. Tuck the root into my bag. Dig for more.

I pluck the pendulous bloom hanging from a bigleaf maple. Shake it clean, flick off a gnat, place it in my mouth, and chew the sweetness. Wander toward the river.

I seek out the sharp needle spines of devil's club and dig. Round river stones and rich black muck. Dig. Cold shock of river water. Dig. I locate fingerlike rootlets and coarse branching roots, then find the joint and cut. Pull it to the light. I choose a jagged broken rock to scrape away the spines. Carve away a flake of bark to reveal mint green inner bark, the medicine. Tuck the root into my bag.

I feel a sudden itchy sting at my ankles and look down to see new spring nettles emerging. I didn't bring gloves, but can't resist free organic greens, healthier than spinach, healthier than kale. I pick carefully, using cottonwood stained thumb and forefinger to pinch off the uppermost stems and tuck them into my bag.

My hands are sticky, soiled, slivered, and stinging. I dip them in the river and let the coolness wash over them, then sit back on a mossy stump. My hands rest in my lap, still.

Grimm's Ducklings

This January dawn a black-capped chickadee lengthened his neck, threw back his head, puffed out throat and cheeks, and sang for all he's worth. Through the closed window I couldn't hear him but I saw him. I watched. An Oreo-striped ping-pong ball atop the lilac, soundlessly singing. I would like to greet my day like *that*.

My bay window overlooking a wooded wetland and my binoculars are often all I need to lift me out of the funkiest of funks. Road rage from rush hour traffic? Look for buttercup-yellow flashes of secretive warblers hawking insects from the willows. Joy returns. Mind racing and overwhelmed by playing extrovert forty hours a week plus overtime? Watch a robin bathe in the shallows—splash, fluff out, and shake off like a puppy. Calm is restored.

Or one of my favorites, the resident Anna's hummingbird. That feathered ornament in the pear tree blinking in the sun. Or rain. Even when still he's anything but—see how his tail rocks slightly, his emerald back rises and falls with the effort of galloping heart and fluttering lungs. Obsidian tweezer bill pans this way and that, tongue flicking out like a snake testing, tasting, hypnotizing, back and forth, to and fro: coal black chin then blazing ruby radiance. Black, then ruby. He blinks and flicks and bobs and pans and entrances.

Then he's off! He's up! Rocket launched into the ether directly at the sun and he just might get there but he pauses, wings a blur, back arched, a wee sickle. Not high enough. Zooming higher still, a final pause, and then zing! The dive! Cymbals crash, the flourish, the exclamation point of wind through wings and just when it seems he will hit the tree he lands, gently, puffs his throat out, sings his *zippedy do da*, and returns to panning, blinking, bobbing, and flicking the thinnest of tongues at the sun. And I, just watching, so full of glee I might lift off myself.

Beauty, levity, and grace: the enchantments of watching birds. The Disney fairytale that can make you forget the toil and drudgery of real life.

And yet…

Last spring, early March in the Pacific Northwest, I spied a wood duck family. Vibrant male and drabber female, attentive like all new parents, herding a dozen fluffy yellow cottonballs. The ducklings scooted and skittered, zipped and zoomed over the surface of the water like wind-up toys on linoleum. I peered through my binoculars to see them closer, how they leaned their heads forward and pumped stubby winglets to keep up with Mom and Dad.

Pure joy!

But then, a gray shadow on black stilts. Great blue heron stalking in the shallows. Fishing, I thought. So still. Head cocked, peering down.

Scrutinizing. Calculating.

He shifted, slightly. Bent, faintly.

And struck! Like sword to target, he speared his prey and then gripped, shook, gulped a little, and paused. I turned the knob on the binoculars. Clearer. Something moved at his mouth. Not a fish. Not a snake. Not a crawdad, nor frog. A tuft of yellow cottonball with two tiny webbed feet, soundlessly paddling nothing but air.

I dropped the binoculars. Looked away.

Then. I picked them up. And watched.

Feet paddled air. Gulp.

Still paddling.

Gulp.

Paddling.

And then it was gone. The shadow went still, a bulge in his throat. Wood duck parents swam, eleven ducklings scooted.

What… what was I feeling?

Nothing. Everything.

Out on my pond, parents lost a child. One life ended. Another life was fed. Did the ducks feel grief, or maybe just a vague sense that something dear was missing? Did the heron rejoice, or maybe just note the relief of an urge, a need satisfied? Whether you would grant birds complex emotional responses, basic awareness, or no consciousness whatsoever, what we can know for sure is that for each one, the world was undeniably changed. And still, like the other birds, those left alive bathed. And flew. And sang.

I watched. And remembered.

Beyond the toil and drudgery of the everyday human world, beyond politics and morality and crime and punishment, all the complex ways we big-brained animals harm or heal each other, there are some phenomena all living beings, skin or feather, share. Beyond violence, beyond suffering, and beyond murder, death itself can be simple. Not necessarily joyful or even comfortable, but ordinary. Commonplace even. Eater and eaten, energy exchanged. One thing always becoming another, no body ever fully separate. As we, even we behind the glass, are not separate. To witness this kind of death is to remember this, and to remember is a deeper consolation than even the most jubilant of hummingbirds.

So now, even when nature seems more Grimm than Disney, I grip the binoculars and focus in. Not to escape real life, but to remember it. Only then can I throw back my head, puff out my cheeks and soundlessly sing for all I'm worth.

Elvis Lives

These animals are native to the African continent but have naturalized globally, the most widely distributed of all primates. Highly adaptive and invasive, we are able to thrive in the hottest, driest deserts, or the coldest snowbound mountains, from the temperate grasslands to the arctic tundra. Like the beaver, we alter our environments to suit our needs, which benefits some species and harms many more. Some of the first wanderers originally reached the North American continent via the Bering land bridge.

Those animals evolved at least eight million years before Homo sapiens. They are native to the Old World but have naturalized across the northern hemisphere, the most widely distributed of all corvids. Highly adaptive and intelligent, they have learned to survive in the hottest, driest deserts or the coldest snowbound mountains, from the temperate grasslands to the arctic tundra. Ravens originally reached the North American continent via the Bering land bridge. Probably, they were following us.

We are generally omnivores, though diets vary widely based on local resources and culture. Some populations are almost exclusively carnivorous, others more herbivorous. Some hunt, gather, and consume plants and animals directly from the earth; most barter for food items processed beyond recognition. To consume animal prey we've gotten creative—using combinations of confinement, intricate tools, and selective breeding to subdue and control food animals. Plants, too, we've domesticated, confining to tidy rows in climate-controlled environments. We cache food and other natural resources extensively and aggressively defend it from other animals, including our own kind. These adaptations metastasized our populations from extended families to villages to towns to sprawling cities which seem to have no growth limit. Still, some live the old ways. And others live in between, on the edges, and make their own ways.

They are generally omnivores, though diets vary widely based on local resources and culture. They prefer animal meat when they can get it. Insects, frogs, snakes, bird eggs, nestlings, and mice they subdue easily. To consume larger or faster prey they get creative. Peck out the eyes, crush with heavy tools, hunt cooperatively like wolves, or clean up scraps from the kills of larger predators, like wolves. Or, historically, humans. Ravens will lead wolves to their larger prey animals, a mutually beneficial arrangement. Back when they followed us, when we were small bands of bison hunters or salmon fishermen, perhaps we followed them too.

Ravens cache food extensively and aggressively defend it from other animals, including their own kind. Once more abundant through the western United States, they retreated to the remaining forests and deserts as our cities ballooned. They aren't as interested in the urban trash we create, not as comfortable with our noise and numbers in cities like coyotes and crows are, but they will feed on our road kills. Ravens stick to the edges.

Humans take in the world through our eyes and to a lesser extent our ears, noses, mouths, and skin. Dexterous and whimsical, we can stretch, run, climb, and swim. We can cartwheel, somersault, dance, and sing. Mostly we walk, or sit.

Our bodies feed our minds, shape them into personalities. Sensations become ideas, make us creators, visionaries, orators, planners, teachers, liars, tricksters. We have varied social structures, read subtle body language. We are self-aware.

Ravens take in the world through their eyes, and to a lesser extent their ears, mouths, and skin. Dexterous and whimsical, they can strut, hop, skip, and jump. They can flap, dive, barrel-roll, slide, and mimic. Mostly they walk, or soar.

Their bodies feed their minds, shape them into personalities. Sensations become ideas, make them creators, visionaries, orators, planners, teachers, liars, tricksters. They have varied social structures, read subtle body language. They are self-aware.

~

This animal is native to New England but has ranged throughout the United States. Highly adaptable and migratory in early adulthood, I've inhabited various ecosystems from northeastern hardwoods—red oak, white birch, and sugar maple—to Rocky Mountain conifer and aspen, and ultimately, Pacific Northwest cedar and bigleaf maple. I've skirted the edges of cities such as Washington D.C., Salt Lake City, Denver, Portland, and Seattle, but I'm less comfortable with the noise and numbers in cities and most content on the outskirts or alone in the wild, forested landscapes. Though I've occasionally formed a pair bond, those haven't lasted, and I've tended to be a solitary animal. One year, I landed in an environmental learning center on a mountain lake in the middle of North Cascades National Park.

That animal is native to the Pacific Northwest cedars and bigleaf maples of North Cascades National Park. Even if he didn't wear a red ankle band from University of Washington wildlife biologist, John Marzluff, and even if he didn't sport the name Elvis, we would all have known that he was a character. Like most of his kind hanging around the small, predictable human villages of national parks, he would notice when messy picnickers packed up and left, or when ignorant city folk left anything resembling food visible in their campsites. But Elvis took everything a step further. If you walked away from your backpack, Elvis might show up to investigate. And unlike the chubby chipmunks, Elvis understood and could open zippers. If you left your lunch on the front seat of your car and your windows slightly ajar against the summer heat, you might return to no lunch and no trace of what might have happened to it.

Elvis did have a mate, naturally named Priscilla, and he did occasionally convene with others of his kind for meetings and discussions, but he alone seemed to engage with our human village intimately. He watched us. He sized us up. He learned which chef was a softie and might toss a piece of burnt bacon out the back door of the kitchen despite knowing that feeding wildlife in a National Park is an absolute no-no. He learned which environmental educators would behave appropriately among their students and then surreptitiously drop a bit of dinner's salmon when nobody else was looking.

I worked in the office, a new but rustic-looking wooden beamed beauty more like a mountain chateau than anything that should contain filing cabinets and computers. The entryway and front desk merged into a grand and airy administrative room, all set under a cathedral ceiling sloping toward one towering wall of windows to alpine peaks and the great beyond. From my desk close to the window I couldn't see the mountains, just the sky if I tilted my head back and looked up. Straight out was a gravel walkway between my building another similar wood-beamed hall, a classroom.

Along this walkway between buildings, flocks of fifth graders fluttered through at regular intervals, laughing, shouting, drunk on mountain air, and thrilled to be free from suburban classrooms for a few days. The silence after their passing was louder by contrast.

Along this walkway between buildings, flocks of red crossbills fluttered through during the quiet intervals, foraging bits of gravel to glean minerals and aid seed digestion. Cherry red males and avocado green females, each with a twisted seed-prying beak for opening pine, spruce, and fir cones. Usually they would fly in, chattering, land and hop about, still chattering, and after general agreement that they'd had enough or when the fifth graders were due back, they'd fly off again. The silence after their passing was louder by contrast.

Humans, crossbills, silence. And so it went, until one day, raven.

Thunk, a crossbill body hit the window.

This animal did not think, but ran outside to find a crossbill, still breathing but not moving. I picked him up, held his warmth, used my other hand to shield his glazed eyes to keep him calmer in the dark. I looked up.

That animal with the red ankle band perched on the classroom roof and looked down at me. His black marble eyes found mine, held me there. He waited.

I hesitated, unsure of my next move. But the feel of a faint heartbeat in my hand triggered an ache in my own chest, and then a decision. *No. Go away.*

He did.

I watched Elvis fly away, then snuck around to a sheltered area off the path, tucked the head-injured crossbill onto a mossy perch hidden under the overhang of a log where he wobbled and slumped, then I left him alone to recover or die. Later when I went back to check on him, he jumped to attention and flew away. No raven in sight.

Another day, *thunk*, a crossbill body hit the window.

This animal ran out to find a dead crossbill, still warm, in the gravel. I looked up.

That animal looked down at me. Waited.

I heard the fifth graders coming. Didn't think. Picked up the limp body. No heartbeat. I raised my hand up and showed Elvis. *See?* He tilted his head and eyed the body. He saw.

Follow me. He followed. I walked around the back of the building, placed the crossbill on a tall boulder. I walked a short distance away. He flew down and ate.

Together, we'd learned something new. Raven could spook the crossbills, chase one into the glass. Then wait. Still alive? No use hanging around, the human wouldn't let him have it.

Dead? Great. The human would set the table and raven could dine in peace.

It has been said that the future is human cities and noise and trash and coyotes and crows. That wolves and ravens and small human villages and hermits are animals of the past. Maybe so. But for now, we're still here, on the edges, watching each other, learning from each other, the way we always have.

Menu

Appetizers

Strawberries, plucked straight from the plants at the U-Pick in Avon Connecticut. While your mother moved efficiently down the rows with her bucket, you plopped yourself in the dirt to select only the choicest, perfectly strawberry-shaped, deepest scarlet berries, and then you nibbled them, then and there. As the summer sun freckled your nose and bleached your snarled hair, you savored the shocking sweetness on your tongue. Red juice slid down your throat, dribbled onto your chin, and stained your fingers.

Your mother yelled over *if you eat any more strawberries, you're going to turn into a strawberry*. You squinted over at her to read whether you needed to get up and be a good helper but found her shoulders relaxed, bare arms hugging her basket, and eyes crinkled in a suntanned smile. She twirled in her sundress and returned to picking. You scootched forward on your dirty bottom and dug in for more, entertaining the idea of turning into a strawberry.

Fresh from your garden, just brush off the dirt: a carrot, stubby and sweet, dug from your Massachusetts garden and munched while you waited for the kindergarten school bus. A lipstick red Macintosh apple pulled from your favorite climbing tree in the Connecticut orchard and crunched while you waited for the fourth-grade school bus. Sun-warmed Roma tomato snipped from the vine in the front yard garden of the communal house in Utah to enjoy on the front porch while your housemate played the fiddle. Sugar snap peas pinched off the vines from the communal garden of the ecovillage in Oregon and shared with the chickens nosing around at your feet. Peppermint leaves picked from the spreading patch by your Washington front door, placed in your mouth, chewed slightly, and held on your tongue. You breathed in the cooling, grounding mintiness, the taste of home.

Fresh from the wilds, nature grown: a nibble of salty seaweed gleaned from the rocky edge of an Atlantic island. A mouthful of tart blueberries picked from a rowboat rocking at the shoreline of a New Hampshire lake. A garnish of sweet clover blossoms pinched from a wildflower meadow in the Rocky Mountain foothills. A hearty salad of miner's lettuce, dandelion greens, chickweed, bigleaf maple flowers, and salmonberry flowers still glistening with dew from one feral Washington backyard.

Eating directly from the earth, you remember that you are always home. And, that you were never separate. That to be alive means to sustain yourself on other lives. Forest leaf, flower, or fruit becomes animal flesh. By the most elemental, scientific definition, you are what you eat.

A La Carte

Anadama bread, warm and steaming from the oven. A New England bread of whole wheat flour, cornmeal, and molasses, kneaded and baked by your father, *A bread of our people for generations*, he said. Your ancestors in England or Scotland likely made bread from oats, barley, and rye. Their ancestors thousands of years before that may have ground ancient grains by hand, mixed them with water, and left them out in the open air to collect wild yeasts and rise before baking them over their hearth fires. Before that? Plant root starch pounded and baked into flatbreads. Daily bread. Bread of life.

Cheese plate, all your favorites. Crumbly extra-sharp Vermont cow's-milk cheddar, smooth creamy spreadable goat cheese blended with garlic and herbs, hunks of nutty, buttery sheep's-milk manchego. One bite will transport you to a pastoral meadow, perhaps the flood-plain valley of your Washington commute, the rocky pasture on the walk to your Connecticut school bus, or a heather moorland from your ancestral past.

In those moorland pastures of Great Britain and northern Europe, generations of your ancestors incrementally gained the ability to digest milk beyond infancy, and therefore to utilize the nutrient-rich elixir cultured from meadow grass and sweet clover, further cultured and preserved to last through the dark northern winters when fresh foods were scarce. Every bite of cheese is a communion with plants, ruminants, bacterial cultures, and ancestors.

Entrees

Largemouth Bass, you caught. You threaded the earthworm onto the hook just like your stepdad taught you, cast your line from the rowboat into Schroon Lake just like he taught you, let out line and slowly reeled it in like he taught you, then, when you felt that tug of life on the other end, you jerked your pole back and reeled in fast, just like he taught you. You felt that fish fight through the line that connected you, and you fought back, strong and stubborn like your family raised you. Though your stepdad would gut and filet it and your mother would beer batter and fry it, you brought home dinner that evening. At nine years old, you discovered the deep satisfaction of feeding your family.

Chicken, you helped kill. You didn't physically end his life, but you held him. First close to your body, stroking his warm feathers and cooing until he fluffed out and shut his eyes in contentment. Then, grasping his ankles with one hand, you slowly turned him upside down and stretched his neck out with the other. Your friend sliced, quick and clean, and you held strong while he twitched, you watched while he bled out onto the earth, you felt as he grew still. When it was done you plucked him, cut him, removed his insides, rubbed his naked body with butter and herbs, and roasted him over the fire. Succulent juices slid down your throat and dribbled onto your chin as you welcomed the bird into your body, to become part of you.

Linguine in cream sauce, after your outdoor school survival trip. After five days eating only the raw materials of the earth—salmonberry shoots, miner's lettuce, violet leaves, fire-roasted nettles, and oyster mushrooms, a bite of charred garter snake—foods which nourished you but never fully satisfied you, you wanted to indulge like a modern human animal again. It looked strange at first, that plate of food fully transformed and unrecognizable as wheat and milk. And yet, as you slurped up mouthful after mouthful of steaming hot creamy smooth pasta, you practically purred with pleasure and gave thanks for the human ingenuity that seeks to feed more than just our physical bodies.

And still, after five days of communing with the forest, you remembered. That recognizable or not, all you ate was once of a living being. That there is no eating without killing—animal, plant, bacteria. Herbivore, carnivore, omnivore, all just different strategies to ingest life, to convert flesh into flesh.

Dessert

Sweets, wherever and whenever you could get them, because your health-nut mother didn't buy junk food. A wad of gum scraped off the street when you were five. Powdered CoolAid licked from the packets brought by friends in the third-grade lunchroom. Twix bars from your friend whose mother actually bought candy. Spoons full of leftover chocolate frosting from the container in the refrigerator after someone's birthday. Sugar cereals at your father's house after the divorce, the more colors and the more marshmallows the better, *don't tell your mother.*

Evolutionary biologists taught us that sugar releases endorphins in our primate brains so that we will seek out and gobble up ripe fruits when available, as sources of quick, easily absorbed energy. We've extracted and concentrated those sugars into colorful chemical doses for exponentially more endorphins. Endorphins alleviate stress, deaden pain, and elicit feelings of euphoria. This junk food for your body is a drug for your mind, and you've been a happy addict all your life.

Ice cream, the ultimate comfort food. The original sustenance, mother's milk, plus added sugar endorphins, cooled and swirled into creamy perfection. In your earliest memory at two and a half, Mom was in the hospital birthing your sister and you were home with Grandma and Grandpa eating ice cream. When you crashed your bike at twelve and busted up your face the first time, you slurped milkshakes with a straw. When a dog annihilated your face for the second time, you returned to milkshakes. Childhood temper tantrums, adolescent brooding, adult mood swings? Ice cream.

In Ayurveda, Chinese medicine, and other disciplines that go beyond nutrients and into the energetics of a food, ice cream cools internal fire, soothes emotional flareups, calms manias. Healing, grounding pleasure by the spoonful. A food, a medicine, for your disposition. Strawberry, pistachio, and coffee were your original favorites. Mint chocolate chip, butter pecan, and rocky road came later. Now, gourmet shops serve up salted caramel, lemon lavender, and bourbon cherry chocolate. You eat it all up; no matter how else your tastes have changed you never tire of ice cream. Your first craving may very well be your last.

Nightcap

You. Spoiler alert—no matter how well you feed your body or mind, whether you give in to hedonistic cravings or cultural body-shaming, the latest food craze or fad diet, no matter what you choose to take in to your body, you will ultimately become food. You have already been on the menu all your life, not just the harmful viruses and bacteria that invade periodically, but the living microbiome inside and out, all the time, digesting your food and you. Your body, your mind, your idea of separateness is only a half-truth. What keeps you alive is your capacity to pass the earth through your body, always changing, never the same.

And when you stop eating, stop ingesting, digesting, and voiding as a unified identity, you will, one way or another, disburse back to earth. And little by little, all that was your body will become parts of other beings, other lives.

So, while you can, eat up.

Alarming

The birds' wisdom is their awareness, and their awareness is their wisdom.

—Jon Young, *What the Robin Knows*[16]

The song sparrows had stopped their Beethoven-esque songs and were harshly chirping. Robins were cheeping. Swainson's thrushes were twanging and towhees were tweeing. I heard them from inside and went out to investigate.

It looked like a peaceful spring day—grass greening up and nearly ready to mow, salmonberries ripening in the thicket, bigleaf maple and cottonwood leaves finally filling out the forest among the evergreens. If my windows had been closed I might not have noticed anything awry. But they weren't, and I had. I heard.

I tilted my head to discern the direction of the ruckus then wandered down my gravel driveway and across the field toward the forest. Something big was going down, and I couldn't ignore it.

I didn't use to hear bird alarms. I was a bird watcher from an early age, but aside from the few songs I recognized and enjoyed like the perky cardinal's, the chatty catbird's, and the haunting veery's, I didn't listen to birds. Bird song—the flirty pronouncements of randy males (and in some species, females)—was just a pleasing backdrop to a spring day.

Only in middle adulthood after a course on "bird language," which combined multi-cultural indigenous knowledge with modern scientific research, did I realize how much more birds are saying. Soft *seets* and *cheeps* between mated pairs or flocking birds to keep tabs on each other while foraging. Plaintive begging calls from nestlings and fledglings, always accompanied by the open-mouthed wing trembling urgency of *feed me now*! Dramatic territorial spats, usually between males, reminiscent of playground posturing or in more extreme cases, bar fights. Typically ignored by other species.

Which brings us to alarm calls. Alarm calls are never ignored, by anyone. Not the other nearby birds, related or not, because the danger may affect them too. Not the nearby mammals, who may also be fearful prey or, if predators, will want to know if they've lost the element of surprise. Or, if they can recognize they aren't the cause of the alarm, they might attempt to use the distraction to their own advantage. Even those tiny-brained amphibians the frogs are paying attention. Pretty much everyone with ears attends to what the birds have to say when they are alarming. **Everyone.**

Everyone, that is, aside from most of us humans.

I was getting closer; the alarms, louder. Loudmouth jays joined in squawking so I knew they couldn't be the danger as they often are. In the dense leafy forest I couldn't decipher the focal point of calls, as both ground birds and treetop birds seemed upset. The alarming was so loud and extensive I couldn't hear beyond to where other birds were unworried and still singing. Everyone seemed annoyed, angry, frightened. I could feel it in my own nervous system, noticed my own breath coming faster and my heart pounding. I found myself looking over my own shoulder, as if something might be after me, too.

Was I stupid to walk toward the danger, against the warnings? Couldn't danger to them be dangerous to me too?

It could, perhaps. But not likely in that checkerboard Cascades foothill forest above a tame farming river valley. My own discomfort bordering on fear was something different, something in my DNA left over from our ancestors, all of whom, when you go back far enough, were not the top of their food chains. Back when we needed to know where our predators might be, as well as how to be sneaky enough to hunt our own food. Back then, we all listened to the birds. Our lives depended on it.

Birds aren't the only announcers by which to measure the pulse of a forest (or field, or jungle, or savannah). Squirrels, prairie dogs, monkeys, frogs, and various other vocal species are worth listening to for their unique reactions to perceived danger. Have you ever stood near a wetland thrumming with frog songs, only to hear them all shut up in an instant? What do they know that we don't? What have they heard, or felt, or sensed in a way we can't even fathom? Other animals probably know the answer. We probably used to.

There are still some cultures living close to the land like the descendants of our Bushmen ancestors, cultures some would call primitive, who still teach, understand, and know bird language. Whose children hush instantly and look up when a monkey screams a particular warning. People who've never forgotten. The rest of us must relearn. But though our brains struggle, our modern languages often inadequate, our bodies remember these older languages easily.

My gut feelings couldn't seem to make up for my other weakened animal senses; I couldn't find the source of the alarms. So I returned to my yard, sat outside with my binoculars nearby, and opened a book to read. But I couldn't focus through the noise, couldn't relax when everyone else was so upset. How had I lived into my thirties without hearing this? I'd often lived surrounded by forests teeming with birds and other animals that eat birds, so this must have gone on. Dramas broadcast in surround sound for all to hear. Now, I hear it all the time.

Could I just decide to unhear it so I might enjoy that peaceful spring day? I couldn't. It wasn't peaceful anymore. I trained my binoculars toward the area of the disturbance and waited.

Aside from the primal need to locate danger, attending to bird alarms has led to exciting discoveries I wouldn't otherwise have had. A coyote sneaking through my suburban yard in broad daylight, newly fledged screech owlets on the edge of a North Cascades lake at dusk, a barred owl sleeping high in a cedar in a city park. I've learned to recognize the robin's thin, high-pitched whistle used mainly for aerial predators, and looked up to spy a silent eagle or hawk I wouldn't have otherwise seen. I once heard my local song sparrows shriek much louder than they ever had at my approach, and looked closer to see a long-tailed weasel pop out from behind a blueberry bush. And I now recognize how my own distracted blundering on a forest trail affects those around me, how I can maintain the peace just by paying attention to the birds. By seeing them, choosing to change direction rather than scaring one up from the path, choosing not to *be* the disturbance.

That robin on the lawn in front of you, who just lifted his head as you approached? He's watching you, waiting to see whether you will act with respect or with apathy. If you seem not to see him, he will likely speak up. Hello? I'm here. *tut tut tut.* HELLO? Don't you hear me?? *Cheep! Cheep!*

And if you continue, he is likely to release an exasperated whinny and fly up and out of your path, using up valuable energy which means more foraging will be required before nightfall. In the wild, every action is measured, necessary. Once you know this, once you begin to hear this, you can't unknow or unhear it. You will feel any unrest you cause. You will see them looking at you. You will hear them protest. If it's gone this far before you wake up, you may feel the need to apologize.

We modern humans haven't removed ourselves from relationship with the natural world. We just changed the roles we play. According to bird language expert Jon Young, "the natural world is a culture of vigilance based on carefully tended relationships and connections, maintained through recognition, mutual respect, and 'jungle etiquette' that in the end preserves the baseline and conserves energy."[17] I may be more of an outsider than my ancestors ever were; I may be mainly a visitor to the wilderness, but shouldn't that mean I should be even more respectful? Shouldn't common human decency extend to more than just other humans?

Respect aside, when I'm wandering in the forest I want to discover the owl above me. I want to look around to see the coyote watching me. And I want to see all the songbirds, hear them singing, not be the cause of alarm. I don't want nature to hide from me.

Maybe you don't feel the need to respect non-human animals and you don't care to see them; are there other reasons to rekindle awareness in the wild? How might it affect our brains?

As hunter-gatherers, our awareness evolved both as predator and prey. Maybe hunting took cunning and brainpower, scavenging certainly did, but fear is an extremely powerful motivator, both individually and evolutionarily. Intense fear stimulates the reptile brain into action—fight or flight. But mild fear, or we might say heightened awareness, inspires creative thinking. A brief or temporary adrenalated state makes the whole world brighter, louder, more present. Your brain is stimulated, more ready to learn from your experience.

An article on NPR's Science web page recounts recent anthropological research suggesting that we may have developed some of our sensory awareness specifically due to this fear. Anthropologist Lynne Isbell's snake-detection theory "posits that the possibility of death or injury from contact with snakes was an evolutionary selection pressure that put our lineage on its path toward visual acuity and highly developed brains."[18]

So, if "the birds' wisdom is their awareness," what *is* our wisdom? What good is consciousness if we are not aware of the world around us? I mean more than just tuning in to our five senses. What about the sixth, that we've nearly lost?

Wild animals (and most tame ones too) pick up on the moods of those around them. Wander into the forest already nervous, or worse, angry, and the animals will know it. Say you are infuriated, cursing and fuming over your job or politics or a fight with your partner—that robin who earlier chided you for obliviousness would likely dive for cover long before you approached. An agitated human may as well be the big bad wolf, out to huff and puff and blow their forest down. "A nervous wolf— a nervous anything—radiates waves of tension that every other creature in the wild senses."[19] Call it woo-woo new-agey vibration nonsense if you'd like, but once you start paying attention in the wilds, you will know this to be true. Anyone with a dog, anyone who's ridden a horse might agree— our animals can sense our moods. Perhaps they are motivated by their personal connections to us, which can be a strong motivator. But wild animals have strong motivations too—to stay alive. To eat and not be eaten. If something nearby is angry, snarling, growling, you'd want to know as soon as possible.

Maybe fear of being eaten evolved animal brains enough, heightened awareness enough for that woo-woo sixth sense to develop. The ability to read moods between species and without common language, without what we would call language at all. If dogs and horses and birds and other beasts have it, surely our big-brained ancestors did. Some of us, arguably, still do. Most, unless we deliberately practice and hone this sense, do not. Or at least we are so out of touch with it that it no longer serves us.

Is our relative safety in the natural world de-evolving us? Is human insularity making us stupid, a sort of Homo sapiens inbreeding? That can't be quite right, as there is certainly no shortage of danger and fear in the human world. In fact we seem to be getting more afraid of each other as years go by (or maybe the current political milieu is clouding my vision). So put another way, does our lack of animal predators, of wild sources of fear that evolved us cause us to seek out danger elsewhere, make us more apt to see danger where it is not? Are we more likely to fall prey to government scare tactics, for example? How might our dearth of wild predators impact the various ways we predate each other?

I'm not saying I wish we could go back to the good old days when we were eaten by lions. Not quite. But I do wonder what we've lost, and what might be breaking down or malfunctioning in our brains and bodies in our relative safety in the natural world. A safety that means that even though I might feel the anxiety in bird alarms, I don't need to act. Don't need to quickly decipher the cause and severity of alarm and determine in an instant the best way to respond to save my life, and I don't need to worry about where my loved ones are and whether they are safe. I don't need to do anything at all. I could go back inside and ignore that whole forest drama. Focus exclusively on the human ones.

But.

The birds were screaming. It was red alert out there. *Mayday! Mayday!* Robins screamed the loudest, screeching like banshees. Everyone else joined in but the robins were shrieking. And suddenly I knew, not in my brain but my body, I knew that someone was getting eaten. Probably, someone's baby.

With dread in my heart, I trotted back toward the woods and as I got closer I heard something else, the swish of thick wings and then the heavy *woof woof woof* of a large bird flying away. I looked up to see a raven, something pale pink in its mouth. Pale pink, still naked. Someone's baby. Robins screamed.

Once you hear it, you can't unhear it. Once you feel it, you can't unfeel it. But that's a good thing, I believe. Tuning in to nature may no longer be necessary for our safety from predators, but I do still think it's important, maybe even essential for our survival as a species. Maybe what this most primal sense taught us, what this wild sensitivity nurtured into a sixth sense, was nothing more than empathy. Not respect or sympathy, a feeling toward something else. Not empathy for our own kind, but empathy for the other. Feeling in our own bodies the energy of a complete stranger. Even another species. Others who may be different from us, but other living breathing singing thriving lives, just the same.

When we can no longer feel or even hear the screaming right outside our own front doors, what then?

Thy Neighbor as Thyself

Anthropomorphism:
1. *"the attribution of human characteristics or behaviour to a god, animal, or object."*
—Oxford English Dictionary

2. *"an interpretation of what is not human or personal in terms of human or personal characteristics"*
—Merriam Webster Dictionary

If I didn't pay them a visit first thing in the morning I would hear about it all day long. I can't quite remember how it came to that, only that one day I decided to bring some peanuts to share. The peanuts weren't specifically for them, they were for everybody, but they found them first and weren't into sharing. The next day I brought more—I'd bought a whole bag—and it sort of became a habit. They came to expect it. Expect me, with peanuts. As soon as I stepped out my front door one of them would notice, would tell the others, and I had better be on my way to the forest edge with peanuts or all hell would break loose, at least among the jays.

It's happened before; I should have expected it. At my cottage in Washington's North Cascades I was a little lonely so I'd started talking to them, those conspicuous extroverted birds, and eventually, they'd started calling out to me too, a strange prattling dialect they seemed only to use with me. Their name for me, perhaps. And my apartment on the outskirts of Portland Oregon where I first started sharing peanuts one winter, because who couldn't use a little more healthy fat and protein in the days of rain and darkness? They got there first, of course, and stayed longest. Came back for more. Asked politely, sometimes, other times demanded.

I know, other people call them trash, call them loudmouth pests, curse when they move into the neighborhood. And yes, they do have raucous parties, and sometimes seem to yell and scream for no reason at all. But if you stick around and look closer, pay attention at the quiet times, you'll see their other side. When they couple up in early spring, watch them nuzzle and preen each other's punkrock 'do's, listen to their gentle cooing sweet talk when they think nobody's watching. See how they pamper their children with tender care and utmost bravery, defending their unkempt knock-kneed tots from the fiercest cats, long after they've left the nest. When I wandered into the forest under their watch to place peanuts on the mossy log we agreed was their table, they'd chatter and giggle in delight then glide down on electric blue wings to collect their treats.

> *Between two men the two abysses are, in principle, bridged by language. Even if the encounter is hostile and no words are used (even if the two speak different languages), the existence of language allows that at least one of them, if not both mutually, is confirmed by the other. Language allows men to reckon with each other as with themselves ...*
>
> *No animal confirms man, either positively or negatively. ... Always its lack of common language, its silence, guarantees its distance, its distinctness, its exclusion, from and of man.*
>
> –John Berger, from "Why Look at Animals"[20]

Other neighbors I saw less often than the jays, but we got to know each other nonetheless. The weedy field and adjacent forest where I lived was just a small segment of the area these graceful beings called home; they moved through with the seasons.

In spring extended families of up to eight circled the verdant meadow munching new nettles, dandelion greens, and maple seedlings. After a meal they sprawled around still chewing, idle royalty overseeing their kingdoms. Sometimes they allowed me to perch nearby, if I moved slowly and sat quietly. If they stiffened and glared at me, wary, I needed only bow my head and speak softly to calm their nerves. Two spritely spotted tykes pranced circles around the adults while Momma looked on proudly.

Late summer I watched mothers with their teenagers. One had her hands full with two young bucks, bodies filling out, hormones they didn't quite know what to do with yet. At twilight in the midst of grazing on clover and blackberries one suddenly rose up and headbutt the other, velvet crowns locking for long moments until they separated and stood twitching and huffing, looking confused and somewhat embarrassed. Mom sidled up to one son; she was cautious, deferent, now smaller than they. Not quite looking at him, she inched her face toward his until their noses touched. He sighed, muscles relaxing, head bowing back to the ground to resume breakfast. She glided over to the other son, touched noses. He calmed. Peace was restored.

> *Anthropomorphism was the residue of the continuous use of animal metaphor. In the last two centuries, animals have gradually disappeared. Today we live without them. And in this new solitude, anthropomorphism makes us doubly uneasy.*
>
> *The decisive theoretical break came with Descartes. Descartes internalized, within man, the dualism implicit in the human relation to animals. In dividing absolutely body from soul, he bequeathed the body to the laws of physics and mechanics, and, since animals were soulless, the animal was reduced to the model of a machine.*
>
> –Berger

In fall I awoke to a dry clacking sound like children's plastic building blocks and looked out to see two large figures, heads together. One sprang up from all fours and pranced away, down the hill behind my cabin around a loop and back up the hill by the other, who watched, still. He repeated this heavy prancing, a stomping dance around and back two more times before returning for one last turn at antler clacking. Heads locked, slow motion pushing and pulling, moving together toward one, then the other, fluidly, like waves cresting and receding. Just as suddenly the act was over; the two disengaged and moved together up into the orchard. I wouldn't see them in the open again until next year. They disappeared during hunting season. Somehow they knew.

In winter I mostly saw the females and younger yearlings crunching forgotten apples in the orchard. But early one January morning as I sat in the cedar grove adjacent to our meadow, footsteps on frozen leaves crunched closer. I saw her first, shy and tentative, traveling a wide circle around the open understory of ferns and mossy logs. She only eyed me sideways.

Then louder crunching. Closer. When he came around the side of the giant cottonwood on the edge of the grove I gasped at his size, super-hero chest and rippling leg muscles marching my way. I looked up the trunk of his body to find a thick neck, white nose, charcoal eyes, and sprawling many-branched antlers. He came within fifteen feet of where I sat, cowering, and his eyes found mine. Searching. Questioning. I dropped my eyes and my head, spoke softly. *I mean you no harm.*

He stalked away, but not far. Stood to the side so I could see the full length of his burly body. He turned to look at me one more time before gazing out through the forest in the direction I was looking. Through the darkness of the cedar grove, through the purple light of naked maples and cottonwoods beyond, towards the glow in the east. We watched the sun rise in silence, together.

> *…animals are always the observed. The fact that they can observe us has lost all significance.*
>
> *Therein lies the ultimate consequence of their marginalization. That look between animal and man, which may have played a crucial role in the development of human society, and with which, in any case, all men had always lived until less than a century ago, has been extinguished. Looking at each animal, the unaccompanied zoo visitor is alone. As for the crowds, they belong to a species which has at last been isolated.*
>
> –Berger

The song sparrow who lived in the stunted apple tree above the blueberry patch was frantic. I'd been sitting in the yard with my back to him, facing out across the meadow with my book and binoculars handy because that was usually the view with the most going on. Warblers and tanagers flitted through the cottonwoods; jays, crows, and occasionally ravens caused their signature corvid ruckus; blacktail deer skirted the edges and every once in a while, especially at dawn or dusk, a bold coyote or one time, a bobcat, golden eyes appearing above the tall grass. It was a pretty happening neighborhood. You know those geezers who sit on their front porches surveying the activity on the street, keeping tabs on the 'hood? *Hi Lloyd, how's your back? Morning Ruth, how are the grandkids? Lovely weather we're having, wouldn't you agree?* That's totally going to be me. Already is, aside from my day job.

But that song sparrow behind me? Frantic. His alarm call was especially piercing, like the squeal of a continually surprised child. So, I turned around. No other trees close by, nowhere for a raptor or corvid to perch. The neighbors didn't have a cat, and there was no place for a larger predator to hide right there. I didn't hear any other alarm calls off in the forest, just the sparrow, right there in the little apple tree above the blueberry patch, freaking out.

I remained oriented in his direction and returned to my book. Then, movement caught my eye. On the ground near the base of one of the blueberry bushes, in a gap in the black strips of weedcloth, something small and brown stood up, facing me.

> *Our look was as if two lovers, or deadly enemies, met unexpectedly on an overgrown path when each had been thinking of something else: a clearing blow to the gut. ... It emptied our lungs. It felled the forest, moved the fields, and drained the pond; the world dismantled and tumbled into that black hole of eyes.*
>
> —Annie Dillard, from "Living Like Weasels"[21]

Morning weasel! Lovely weather we're having, wouldn't you agree? She stood taller as if to see me clearer, a Slinky defying gravity. Ginger belly to the sunshine, arms at her brunette sides, blonde hands and fingers held gracefully, a debutante in elegant fawn gloves. She looked at me briefly and with only mild interest then back down at the weedcloth where something much more interesting awaited. A family of mice perhaps, or a snake? She disappeared. I returned to my book.

Over the next hour she reappeared multiple times, the sparrow repeatedly shocked anew. Up next to one blueberry bush, and gone. Up next to the metal stake holding down the weed cloth, she stretching tall next to it as if to climb it, then flash! Disappeared. Curious, sneaky, playful, stealthy; pop goes the weasel!

> *What does a weasel think about? He won't say.*
>
> —Dillard

Sparrow never calmed down. Nor would I if there was a weasel in my house who was big enough to eat me in one gulp. Weasel mostly seemed to ignore him, as she did me. There was weedcloth to play under, mole tunnels to explore, and the smell of rabbits in the blackberry thicket nearby. The feel of sunshine on her belly and the warm earth under the pads of her feet. I had a book to read, birds to watch, the smell of cottonwoods in the forest nearby. The feel of sunshine on my face and the warm earth under the pads of my feet. We each went about our business.

Later, as I walked around the other side of the house toward my door, she popped up almost at my feet. Looked up at me. I looked down at her. *See you tomorrow, then?* She disappeared under my house.

> *I don't think I can learn from a wild animal how to live in particular... but I might learn something of mindlessness, something of the purity of living in the physical senses and the dignity of living without bias or motive. The weasel lives in necessity and we live in choice...*
>
> —Dillard

Those clowns didn't seem to be worried about our long-tailed weasel neighbors; they were frolicking in the yard again. The two bigger ones played leapfrog in the clover, taking turns at jumping up and over each other, noses wiggling all the while. Then they flopped down on their sides, bellies to the sun, grooming like cats.

The small bunny with the white spot on his nose kicked up dust in the gravel driveway, a kid in the sandbox. Maybe he felt left out, because he kept sneaking over to one of the bigger kids, nipping at his rear, then retreating under my car. Either they had had enough of his shenanigans or perhaps they realized they'd been in the open long enough; the older ones eventually retreated across the yard to the safety of the blackberry thicket. White spot beelined for the blueberry patch.

> *Flopsy, Mopsy, and Cottontail, who were good little bunnies, went down the lane to gather blackberries; but Peter, who was very naughty, ran straight away to Mr. McGregor's garden…*
> —Beatrix Potter, from *The Tale of Peter Rabbit*[22]

I was worried because I'd seen the weasel recently and I couldn't see the blueberry patch from my window, so I headed outside and around the house to see. There was no sign of Weasel but I spied White Spot, who froze with big frightened eyes. I averted my own eyes and spoke softly to calm him but to no avail. Big eyes, nose not twitching at all. Frozen. Song sparrow witnessed the tension and chirped in alarm.

> *Peter gave himself up for lost, and cried big tears; but his sobs were overheard by some friendly sparrows, who flew to him in great excitement, and implored him to exert himself.*
>
> –Potter

When I dropped my head and turned to the side he made a break for it, running—not hopping—across the open meadow toward the blackberry thicket on the edge of the fir forest. I pictured him reuniting with his mother, flopping down exhausted. Mother nuzzling him, relieved and a bit exasperated.

> *Peter never stopped running or looked behind him till he got home to the big fir-tree. He was so tired that he flopped down on the nice soft sand on the floor of the rabbit-hole, and shut his eyes. His Mother was busy cooking; she wondered what he had done with his clothes. It was the second little jacket and pair of shoes that Peter had lost in a fortnight!*
>
> –Potter

I was raised on Beatrix Potter books. *The Tale of Jemima Puddleduck*, *The Tale of Mrs. Tittlemouse*, and of course, *The Tale of Peter Rabbit*. Of course I knew that rabbits didn't wear clothes. Of course I knew that rabbits didn't speak English. But the stories of their lives, their joys and fears and adventures? I assumed, as most kids would, that they were real. Could happen. Probably did.

Then I grew up. And understood, as most adults would, that Beatrix Potter's stories consisted of humans dressed in animal skins meant to entertain and teach children the proper ways to behave in human society. They weren't animal stories at all, just human parables. Anthropomorphism.

Western religions, science, and pop culture all taught me that we are so unique, so special, blessed, highly evolved, etc., as to be completely separate from all other life on earth. Humans may have been animals, once. But no longer. To grow up in our culture is to learn we are alone.

> *We tend to see wild animals less, but love the idea of them more. 'The urge to turn animals into either things or into people reflects the distance we have traveled in a generation or two', writes Stephen Budiansky in The Covenant of the Wild, ... 'We conveniently alternate between anthropomorphism and blindness.'*
>
> *Since animals are a silent majority, and we can only ever project (onto) them, how do we negotiate between anthropomorphism and blindness so as to least marginalize them between the margins of our writing?*
>
> –Nick Neely, from "Why Write About Animals"[23]

Someone cut down my hammock. Why would someone cut down my hammock? It'd been up less than a week, in the cedar grove near my house. I'd bought some fairly expensive webbing fasteners that looped around the trees so as not to hurt them, but someone slashed through one of them leaving one end of my hammock lying on the ground. There, five parallel cut marks on the cedar tree, as if with an ax. Why would someone cut down my hammock?

> ... *they are the closest of all animals to humans. Everybody says, 'After you take a bear's coat off, it looks just like a human.' And they act human: they fool, they teach their cubs (who are rowdy and curious), and they remember. They are confident. They will eat little trifles, or knock down a moose, with equal grace. Their claws are delicate and precise: they can pick up a nut between two tips. They make love for hours. They are grumpy after naps. ... They are forgiving. They can become enraged, and when they fight it's as though they feel no pain. They have no enemies, no fears, they can be silly, and they are big-hearted. They are completely at home in the world. They like human beings, and they decided long ago to let the humans join them at the salmon-running rivers and the berryfields.*
> –Gary Snyder, "The Woman Who Married a Bear"[24]

I felt foolish when I realized a human had not cut down my hammock. Ecology degree, environmental educator, wildlife tracking training, even a neighbor's stories of a bear dismantling the fence around his garbage cans, then his beehives, and I had no clue. I'd lived there in that feral river valley outside of Seattle nearly a year and hadn't seen one, nor any evidence of one. Until, that is, the resident bear decided she didn't like the placement of my hammock in her cedar grove.

When I finally figured that out, I saw evidence of her everywhere. Broken, bent, and healed over branches in the neighbor's apple tree. Nibbled and scarred-over bases of cedar and cottonwood trees from where she'd fed on the sweet inner bark. Rotting stumps torn apart and shelf mushrooms knocked off downed trees from where she'd hunted grubs and beetles. And on that hammock tree? Older scratches, bite marks, and a couple hairs. It was clearly her tree, her signpost that I'd so rudely usurped, and she wasn't having it. Point taken, eventually. I moved my hammock to the other side of the grove.

She left it there, allowed my presence there, and though I returned often to that cedar grove I saw only the jays and deer and other residents. After the hammock incident I didn't see any fresh bear sign in the area until winter left an impressionable white sheet on my driveway, and I happened to wander down it before it melted. The driveway was a forested half-mile, rock and gravel winding up from the river valley below to an open meadow above. On either side, steep ravines with seasonal streams cut through a mixture of coniferous cedar/

fir and deciduous maple/cottonwood, with plenty of brushy shrubby undergrowth providing food and shelter for a variety of animals.

And on that snowy morning there she was, or had been recently. Like a giant, flat-footed human walking barefoot. Bear foot. Perfect footsteps melted into the snow by warm feet. Up from the ravine and down the driveway for a ways and into the woods on the other side. Back up the driveway paralleling the other steps and then surpassing them, continuing up toward the cedar grove. I followed them. Down, across, back up, and through. I walked with her.

I lost her tracks in the woods where the snow hadn't touched the ground, but followed with my eyes and imagined where she was then. Her den probably, back to dozing after her winter outing on that relatively warm Pacific Northwest morning. I hadn't seen her, might never see her, but I was getting to know her nonetheless.

Blackberry season rolled around, and though after years of battling that most aggressive invasive exotic with shovel, shears, machinery, and fire, on that rented property in a raggedy meadow we came to a tentative truce. For a month or so, everyone would be stained with wine-red juices. Jays left purple scats on the mossy log. Bunnies and Deer feasted at their respective face levels, and their predators knew to seek them there.

Sun-warmed blackberries atop vanilla bean ice cream is one of my greatest joys of summer, and worth all the scratches I get from trying to reach the biggest, juiciest ones. So, there I stood one rare ninety-degree almost humid August day, when out from a thicket nearby trundled a large black beauty. She looked at me, and I at her.

Hi bear. What an honor to finally meet you! You are not surprised to see me, are you? You knew I was here, know me better than I know you, don't you? I spoke softly, mustering equanimity.

She looked behind her, then back at me. I looked across the meadow at the front door of my cabin, and back at her, then down at my feet. My heart beat fast—she was really big—but I stood still.

She walked on, across the meadow. Looked behind her again. Out tumbled a miniature version of her, stubby-legged, giant feet, and wide eyes. I kept my eyes down, didn't move.

He trotted after Momma, caught up to her. She walked on, steadily but confidently, unhurried. They disappeared in the woods on the other side.

For a long time only the bears and birds were at the berry thickets and the rivers. The humans arrived later. At first they all got along. There was always a bit of food to share. Small animals might be as powerful as big ones. Some, and a few humans, could change skins, change masks. ...

The human beings in the original time weren't so bad. Later they seemed to drift away. They got busy with each other and were spending all the time among themselves. They quit coming to meetings, and got more and more stingy. They learned a lot of little stuff, and forgot where they came from.

–Snyder

I sat in the chair in my yard, book and binoculars on my lap, listening to the wind in the cottonwoods. Especially that giant one rising up from the edge of the cedar grove, crown extending over it as if watching over it. It sounded so much like water lapping at a pebbled shore, a little piece of the river a half-mile below. The wind was picking up in the heat of that late August afternoon, as it does when warm air moves up the valleys into the hills, up into the sky where turkey vultures and eagles spiral up and up until they disappear.

A large gust knocked over my bike from where it was leaning against the house, and it crashed onto a potted rosemary plant. I stood and turned toward the ruckus, and there in my vision a few feet beyond, Baby Bear stood at the edge of the blackberry thicket. Also surveying the ruckus, also surveying me. He tumbled back into the thicket.

I angled my chair to face him. I couldn't see him in the mess of leaves, canes, and berries, but I knew he was there, munching, juice running down his chin. Movement at Baby Bear height, a tug here, a rustle there.

And yet we have so much more in common than these of-the-body needs. We all poop, yes. But we all ponder too, in a manner that may or may not be human but is whole and wondrous. We are at every moment surrounded by consciousness, a feast of unique intelligences. Every creature has its particular ways and wiles. Each being has its own presence, voice, silence, song, body, place.

—Lyanda Lynn Haupt, from *Mozart's Starling*[25]

~

It was early twilight, too late for the jays to be seeking handouts, but I went to the forest with peanuts in my pockets anyway. As I deposited my offering on the mossy log, something sailed over me, a cool wind like an ocean current, strong and soundless. I looked up.

Across the open understory of the grove, dark eyes beamed at me from the lowest branch of a young cedar. I held his gaze. Took a few steps backward, still holding, and crouched down next to an old cedar. We remained silent. I breathed, and looked. He looked back. We didn't blink. I wanted to hold him there. Maybe he wanted to hold me too.

And then, he flew, but not away. Directly toward me. He alighted in the lowest branch of the cedar about fifteen feet above me, and looked down. I looked up. Though the forest was darkening, shadows spreading, his eyes shone darker than any of it, two black holes in the center of ringed gray saucers.

The smoky barring pattern on his breast paralleled the cedar bark, so after he ruffled his wing feathers, wiggled his tail, and settled back to stillness he melted into the tree, as if an extension of it, a burl or a knot. Then, he looked out at the forest.

I looked too, imagined seeing as he saw. Hearing as he heard. Feeling the slight breeze ruffle my feathers. Did the world look different, sound different, feel different, then? It did. It does. I was no longer the human I was when I entered the forest. I was not owl either, but some mix of the two. Perhaps he was the same.

> *It's wrong to say that animals do not feel what we feel; indeed, they may feel far more than we do and in far different emotional shades. Given that their senses are often a hundred times more perceptive than ours, could not their emotional equipment be similarly vast?*
> —Brian Doyle, from *Martin Marten*[26]

I feared I was bothering him, disrupting his hunting time, so I crept away toward the far end of the grove and perched next to the cottonwood tree. I expected him to either ignore me and continue surveying the forest or perhaps fly off if I'd disturbed him too much. Instead, he followed. Flew to a maple tree adjacent to my cottonwood, and we gazed at each other again. And suddenly, I relaxed.

I was no longer on edge but calm. I smiled and sighed. It's hard to explain how I knew this, as nothing in his face or visible body language had changed, but I understood that he wasn't bothered, wasn't annoyed with me. He was enjoying the novelty of my presence as I was his. As soon as I consciously realized that, he straightened up and slowly turned around, back to surveying the forest. Listening for the rustle or the squeak that might mean dinner. And I, honored to be offered a seat at the head of the table, remained.

> ... *the things of the world continue to beckon to us from behind the cloud of words, speaking instead with gestures and subtle rhythms, calling out to our animal bodies, tempting our skin with their varied textures and coaxing our muscles with their grace, inviting our thoughts to remember and rejoin the wider community of intelligence.*
> —David Abram, from *Becoming Animal*[27]

The Jays were nowhere to be found; the Deer were scarce. No sign of Weasel or the Rabbits. Bears and Owl were probably hunkered down somewhere dark and cool on that hot and bright summer afternoon. A pair of sparrows chirped quietly to each other and a far off Swainson's thrush spiraled his sweet summer song. Out in the meadow not much seemed to be moving aside from a handful of grasshoppers and a few lazy dragonflies; a turkey vulture spiraled above. But something moved in the forest.

Dried leaves crunched and sticks snapped, somewhere near the cedar grove. Something big and clumsy was marching through. I put my book down to look, but couldn't see through the verdant curtain of cedar, maple, and cottonwood at the edge of the meadow. Then, I heard it.

A motor roared to life, growled and snarled, then howled and wailed, devouring silence. I froze. Sniffed the air—gasoline, maybe a little oil. I stared in vain at the green, gripped the arms of my chair. My heart was beating so fast. Was I scared? Why was I scared?

I knew what it was. Knew who it was. Just a chainsaw. Just the landlord. Maybe he was harvesting wood to build something new—I did live in a wooden cabin he built—or maybe he was doing some thinning, managing the forest for overall forest health and longevity or for species preference —I did understand forest management practices. I'd participated in forest management practices. I'd pulled the plants we call weeds, cleared thickets of undesirable shrubs, cut down trees that weren't where or what we wanted them to be. This wasn't my land. Those weren't my trees. That wasn't my forest. But.

Please not *that* forest. Please not *those* trees. Please, not *this* little piece of land.

I was rooted to the ground, my stomach lead. I clenched my teeth. I watched the trees. I listened to the machine. It was coming from the cedar grove. It was screaming.

And then I saw her. Head and shoulders above the rest, above the mossy log and ferns, above the maples and cedars, stood the grandmother cottonwood tree. She was swaying. Not the swaying I was used to, her shimmying leaves and gentle dance with the wind. This was the dizzy wavering of someone about to collapse.

Her head bobbed forward, first, then lurched back, and she began to fall. And she fell. And fell. And, fell.

The crash was deafening, but not as loud as the subsequent silence.

> *What if like the hunkered owl, and the spruce bending above it, and the beetle staggering from needle to need on that branch, we all partake of the wide intelligence of this world—because we're materially participant, with our actions and our passions, in the broad psyche of this sphere?*
>
> –Abram

Days passed before I returned to the cedar grove. In the once open understory of ferns and mossy logs, broken branches lay at strange angles and clumps of wilting leaves lay still. In places where bark was torn away, the inner cambium had turned red. Stretching across the well-worn path the deer and I had made, through the clearing and beyond into denser forest, lay her long, straight trunk, prostrate.

I hoisted myself up onto her side—even lying down she was tall—and sat with my legs hanging down, my hands flat on rough bark. I felt her below me. The angles were all wrong.

The forest animals were quiet, my cottonwood was quiet, but the standing trees made their music in the wind. Subtle whispers of cedars, percussive clapping of maples, and far off, the rain-song of another cottonwood. I breathed in and smelled the sweet perfume of cottonwood drying in the sun, and realized this particular area of forest hadn't felt sun on the ground for many years. I wondered how that felt for the insect life, the ferns, the moss, and mushrooms. I sat, and breathed, and smelled, and listened, and felt the sun on our skins.

I looked around me, wondering what the forest looked like when she was small. Then I wondered what it would look like in another hundred years. Who would live here then? Not I, nor those particular forest animals, though maybe our descendants. And the cottonwood? She might sprout new growth from her trunk. One of her branches stuck in the ground could take root in that same earth so she could live again, live still. Cottonwoods are magical like that. She could outlive us all.

But maybe not. Maybe that was the end of her particular life. And though Jays might eat her seeds and plant them anew far from there, though Deer and Rabbits might find shelter in the new fortress-like brush pile and Weasel and Owl find new hunting territory there, and though Bear might nibble the sweetness of her inner bark to make it through the winter, that unique individual Cottonwood will breathe no more. Eventually, moss will grow on her trunk which we now call a log and long after that, even that most solid thing will decompose back to soil so that it's hard to tell where she ends and the earth begins.

I lay down, flat on my back with my legs stretched out against her skin. I looked up at the treetops swaying, and at the blue sky through the hole of her absence. When I finally got up to go, I left some peanuts on the cottonwood log. I knew when I returned tomorrow, they'd be gone.

> *Awakening as this upright, wide-eyed, smooth-skinned thing, I noticed that all the other things around me were also awake…*
>
> *—Abram*

Them

I heard them coming. The racket of skateboards on sidewalk is not subtle. *Click click click* over the cracks like train cars on rails. My body stiffened and I hastened to the edge of the gray granite city park that was my responsibility. Spread-legged, arms crossed, and scowling, I squinted in the direction of the offensive noise. Rounding the corner of 9th & Taylor, they came into view and headed directly for me.

They knew they were not welcome. They also knew I would not be able to stop them.

"Excuse me! There is no skateboarding in this park!" I yelled as they weaved around me and into the square. The din amplified as their wheels assaulted the Chinese granite paver stones. One of the boys flicked a lit cigarette at me as he passed, knowing smoking is not allowed either. I stalked after them cursing under my breath, but they outpaced me, howling and jeering. Taking their time traversing the square, they made sure to jump their boards up, on, and over each of the Brazilian Ipe wood benches, turn over a few of the metal chairs and tables I'd just arranged, and splash through the shallows of the fountain before making their way out of the park. I watched them go, my eyes lasers willing one of them to trip and fall but that time, none of them did.

Angry, bitter teenagers. Angry, bitter security guard. We played our roles well.

~

As a way in with Portland Parks that I hoped would land me a job in an actual forested park, I braved the job of "park host" in a newly constructed downtown Portland piazza, Director Park. Instead of enlisting real security guards from a private company like the more strictly controlled Pioneer Courthouse Square two blocks away, Parks & Recreation chose to hire less authoritative, more approachable, more educationally inclined (and cheaper) park hosts.

Between cleaning up after the lunch crowd, attempting to enforce the no-smoking no-skateboarding no-dogs-off-leash no-panhandling rules, and making sure nothing illegal went on in our public bathroom, my job was to stand there, and watch.

~

He was back again, and I was watching him. How could I not? He was strutting his stuff to music only he could hear through his headphones and he was taking up space like a model on a catwalk. Though the sun hadn't yet crested the Paramount Hotel and Fox Tower to the south and east, his shirt was off, revealing the shapely pectoral and abdominal muscles of a barely post-pubescent young man. His hair was a sleek shoulder-length ponytail he whipped in circles as he gyrated his hips and undulated his arms. In a single leap he was up on top of the round fountain centerpiece, striking a pose. I don't know if he was practicing for the show or if that was the show. As far as I could tell, I was the only one watching.

I liked to watch him dance. It was a hell of a lot more interesting than watching the corporate world rush off to work. After the first time, I stopped being embarrassed for him because he clearly wasn't, and he deserved an audience. I wanted to clap at the end of his routine or maybe even tuck a dollar bill into a pocket of his skin-tight jeans, but I didn't.

～

When patrons were amusing me or the park was empty, I didn't mind my job. Northwest rains cleared the place out, leaving me to watch the young yellowwood trees sway in their perfect squares of soil. Or, chase discarded pages of newspapers and napkins swirling with leaves in urban whirlwinds. Leaning against the glass office listening to the house finches nesting in the cracks between the steel pylons and glass canopy above, I would think, not a bad way to make a buck.

Dealing with the grime of a city wore on me, however. Picking up cigarette butts, cleaning blood off the bathroom walls, and sweeping syringes out from behind the toilet made it difficult to remain the positive presence I was hired to be. Even on days when I didn't have to dodge lit cigarettes. Even in my preppy blue polo shirt with its perky collar. Inevitably my welcoming smile got more strained and false as the minutes ticked to hours.

I bonded with others on the block in similar low caste service positions. The punky baristas at the coffee counter on the corner. The sharply dressed valets at the hotel on Taylor and the steakhouse on Park. We shared nods and eye rolls and didn't waste our smiles on each other.

~

They were both wearing grease-stained tan Carhartt overalls and brown work boots, charming on men who looked to be in their sixties. They carried torn and duct-taped external frame packs with sleeping bags attached with bungee cords. Perched on the top of one was a tiny blue-eyed kitten with a twist-tie collar. She couldn't have been more than a month old.

They lowered their belongings down onto the concrete slab wall across from my closet-sized office while one of the men went into the single-occupancy bathroom next door. I came out of my glass fishbowl where I'd been hiding and made a beeline for the kitten.

"Her name is Tyche, for the goddess of luck. I found her in a dumpster," he said as he wiped the few remaining wisps of hair back over his shiny sunbaked scalp and leaned back against the concrete. I grinned and gave the kitten a scratch under the chin. She burst into a big cat purr.

On his forearm was a Celtic knot tattoo like mine, except his was faded to light gray. "We just got off the train," he told me with crinkled eyes and a sad smile. "Up from California, this time. We've been riding the rails for years."

I tried hard to think of something interesting and appropriate to ask that wasn't banal or patronizing, but came up with nothing. I smiled and stroked Tyche.

He was different than the street kids I saw on a daily basis. Seemed tired, but not beaten. Hardened, but not angry. Wise. He was more like my fantasy idea of a hobo than anyone else I had seen. It was the first time I'd ever really wanted to give someone money, but I could have gotten fired for that.

After his friend came out of the bathroom, we nodded at each other and they walked away. A part of me wanted to follow them, to find out what they knew, to find out what a hobo actually is and is not. I never saw them again.

—

I hated being an authority figure. A bright blue Gore-Tex jacket with the words PARK STAFF on it meant security and even police to some people. It meant I was *The Man*. How did a nonconformist free-thinking liberal introvert end up being The Man? She needed a job, that's how. So when a business-suited woman cursed me for asking her not to smoke or a homeless man spit at me for saying he couldn't panhandle within the boundaries of the park, I hated them and hated myself at the same time.

But it wasn't always like that.

—

Not all the street kids were angry. Not him, the early twenty-something boy who spent his days sitting in un-supervised Shemanski Park a couple blocks south holding a cardboard sign. He came to use our bathroom almost every hour. I heard he was selling drugs over there, but I never knew that for sure. I didn't know what he did in the bathroom either but I did know that I could relax around him. He was always polite and never left a mess so I didn't pry, just nodded and smiled.

"What's your name?" he said after a few weeks of this routine.

"It's Heather. Yours?"

"Patrick. It's nice to meet you, officially. Hey, thanks for being nice to me."

"Patrick, thank you for being nice to *me*."

"That's because you were nice to *me* and didn't judge me."

"Because you were nice to *me*..."

We went in a circle like this, beaming at each other, surprised and pleased with ourselves for not playing our expected roles, neither willing to take the credit.

There were others who made me smile. The flute player who lurked in the parking garage underneath the park, a modern-day Pan, making use of the acoustics and privacy of the world below. I liked to take my breaks down there so I could listen. He liked level five.

And the cat man, a lanky weathered cowboy, a real Marlboro man, except with a leashed exotic looking cat on his shoulder. The cat man walked tall with his back straight; the cat stood tall gripping with claws extended into his canvas jacket, and both looked out at the city. Portland royalty. Sometimes he would stop and let me pet the cat. Other times he would just tip his hat and say, "Good afternoon, m'lady." Then I would feel like a princess and it wouldn't even matter that I'd just spent a half-hour wiping blood off the bathroom walls.

~

Can strangers change our lives? Perhaps, if we let them. They can rearrange the way the world makes sense or change the ways we see ourselves, even if only temporarily. Sometimes all it takes is a gentle open-mindedness, a questioning and reworking of roles and attitudes. Other times, a single experience hits like a storm and swirls us together in the wind like the newspapers, napkins, and leaves.

~

I didn't see her go in to the bathroom, but I knew it had been occupied for too long. I banged on the shatterproof frosted glass-plated steel door and hearing nothing, used my key to unlock it. When I pushed in I saw her, lying on the concrete floor next to the steel toilet. Next to a belt and a syringe.

She was dying. Eyes rolled back and eyelids fluttering. Twitching, body tremors, teetering on a grand mal seizure. Her skin color changed from muddy green to blue as her breathing slowed to occasional gasps. I donned the latex gloves I kept in my back pocket, called 911, and knelt down next to her. And held on.

I placed one hand flat on her upper chest, feeling for breath I couldn't see anymore, the other I pressed into the weak pulse of her wrist. I watched her face. I reminded myself to breathe. *Breathe*, I reminded us.

Slowly, her eyes ceased fluttering and her color warmed to pink. I felt her breathing deepen and her pulse strengthen. She was coming back instead of slipping away. I heard sirens.

The door exploded open and suddenly everyone was there—paramedics, police, gawking onlookers. They shoved me into the background. A few minutes later she was awake and somehow standing on wobbly legs. Then she was gone and everyone else went back to where they came from.

I swept up the syringe and put it in the sharps container. Checked for blood and finding none, reopened the bathroom. Only then did I sit down in my gray granite park and attend to my own racing heart and hands that wouldn't stop shaking for an hour.

～

I saw her once after that. She passed me on the sidewalk as I was heading to a movie theater with friends. The sight of her stopped me cold. Skinny, harried, clutching a brown leather bag, she rushed by, leaving me gawking at her retreating figure.

"Do you know her?" my friend asked.

"Well, um, no. I don't. She…" I didn't know her. She was just a girl who played the role of a junkie overdosing. She played it as generically as I've seen it in movies, minus the epinephrine syringe in the heart to shock her awake. I didn't know *her* at all.

But. I was there with her in that bathroom as she fought death. I held her wrist. I felt her heart. We breathed together. For a few brief moments The Man and The Junkie disappeared and we were just two human lives struggling, separately together. That's something, isn't it?

I would like to say that I was able to make peace with my role as park host, that I never again yelled at skateboarders, cursed smokers or narrowed my eyes at street kids. Though I like to think of the interesting characters and memorable events of my tenure in Director Park, the truth is that up to my last day in that blue park staff uniform, I remained for the most part a grumbling authority figure. Only when I handed over that polo shirt and jacket and stepped back into the anonymity of civilian life could I feel free of that weight. Comfortable again in my own skin, and comfortable among the others. Only then could I step foot on the gray granite stones of Director Park and smile for real among all of them.

Alone Together

You tucked into the last available window seat on the light rail train and snugged your feet against the heater. Pressed your forehead against the cool window and looked out into the pre-dawn darkness. Only outlines were visible, line drawings of cottonwood trees along the river and chevrons of lighter sky among inky clouds. You dropped your head and opened your book.

You were reading Nabokov's *Speak Memory* because you heard it was one of the first famous memoirs and you love climbing into other people's brains for a change. You're often surprised to find how different you are from seemingly similar people and how similar you are to those who seem, on the outside, completely different. And there—you learned that even as a young child Nabokov insisted on spending mornings alone, exploring, bushwhacking through the countryside, butterflying. Yes, you thought. Just like you. Different countryside, different butterflies, different time, but yes, alone.

Then you looked up from your book and looked around. Noticed all the different faces, some in the glow of their phones, others tucked into real books—the whisper of a turned page—many plugged into headphones from which faint beats seeped out. Hip hop. Acoustic folk rock. Baroque. Hugging backpacks and briefcases, clutching textbooks and travel mugs. Fifty people, probably, in your field of vision, and nobody was speaking. Not even the teenagers or the young girl in a private school uniform sitting on her father's lap. The heaters hummed and the train rumbled and everyone hushed with the energy of morning.

As the train clicked onto the bridge crossing the river to city center, the cotton candy pink glow of sunrise spilled onto our hair, our shoulders, flowed over us like syrup and one by one we looked up, looked out. The river flickered like firelight and the mirrored skyscrapers flashed red. We watched in silence, together.

―

The surprise of a brass band stopped you in your tracks, as it seemed to have stopped others who were probably on their way somewhere else but were now standing still, well not still exactly because the music was so absurdly cheerful it was hard not to bounce along to it. That surprise sunny day in a long string of rainy gray already had everyone feeling giddy as Pacific Northwesterners do on such days so the addition of the brass band was almost overkill, almost too much to take, and any minute any otherwise refined adult might burst out with a giggle or guffaw or some other unbecoming expulsion of pure joy.

You gave in to it and sat smiling for a spell on a dry patch of red brick wall on the edge of the square. Beyond the band perched a farmer's market where you spied the fiery hues of ripe tomatoes and could smell the basil that wanted to go along with it, perhaps on a crusty heel of bread from the bakery vendor down the lane. As you tapped your foot to the bass drum you searched the familiar market with your mind and planned your moves. You knew the vendors you'd visit, knew their tanned faces and weathered hands.

Tomatoes, basil, and rainbow chard from the tie-die-clad organic farmer with the squinty eyes and dreadlocks. A baguette from the aproned women at the French bakery. Fresh eggs, the kind with rich orange yolks that put the anemic yellow grocery store eggs to shame and a tub of herbed goat cheese that costs more than your thrift store outfit from the fresh-faced artisan dairy farmer who will talk your ear off about his farm if you let him. You'll let him. And maybe, a bouquet of red sunflowers for your yellow kitchen. It was that sort of day.

Back on the brick wall you sneezed and both the white skateboarder who smelled of weed on your left and the black businesswoman who smelled of perfume on your right said *Bless you*, and we continued enjoying the band at the market in the town square in our city.

―

You were lost in Patti Smith's memoir, *M Train*. You enjoyed her reminiscences, the travels she invited you on, brushing shoulders with other famous people or just doting on her cats, but most of all you loved when she hung out in that Greenwich Village café, drinking black coffee, eating brown bread, and not doing much of anything at all. You could stay there for hours with her, and sometimes you did.

When you closed the book, you were almost surprised to find yourself staring at a mocha and a cinnamon scone on a wooden table in a quiet corner of your own favorite café on the opposite edge of the continent. A gust of cold air swirled around your ankles as a wool-clad bearded man stepped in from outside, and you looked out at the darkening silver sky and maple leaves shivering above the street, thankful not to be out there right now. Inside the lamps glowed soft yellow.

Elliot Smith crooned some slow sad acoustic tune over the speakers but with the cheerful hiss of the milk steamer, athletic espresso grinding, someone tapping away at a laptop, and undecipherable calm chatter from the comfy chairs in the back of the shop the energy was light. At one table a lesbian couple fussed over a toddler who insisted on holding his own mug of hot chocolate. At the neighboring table hipster men with skinny jeans and black-rimmed glasses drank black coffee and discussed bands you've never heard of and will likely never hear of because you aren't that cool, which you are finally old enough not to mind. You were content in your baggy jeans, green striped sweater, and lumberjack boots, in your corner with your sweets and your *M Train*. But you were glad they were all there, too. You felt held in that space, part of something, like a family relaxing together on holiday. Albeit a family who doesn't nag or fight and generally leaves each other alone.

There was no actual connection among you, nothing shared aside from the coincidence of that coffee shop at that moment in time. To each other, you were all archetypes of people, the most basic shallow surfaces of individual lives. But sometimes, that can feel more real. We all have secret, unknowable inner lives. We are all, ultimately, alone inside our heads, our bodies. And isn't it nice, sometimes, to be alone together?

~

There must have been over a thousand people there, sprawled on blankets or relaxing in lawn chairs. They'd brought picnics and takeout and probably beer, wine, and cocktails though stealthily in travel mugs and thermoses because that's not allowed on school grounds. Children ran in packs on the edges, sledding down steep grassy hills on flattened cardboard boxes—possibly the only sledding many of those kids would see that year unless their families drove to the snow.

It could have been the scene of a summer concert or a sports event and in a way it was both. It's just that the event was not of human design, not human driven at all. That old elementary school hosts an old brick chimney that as a stand-in for a hollow dead tree is one of the most popular nighttime roosting locations for, at peak, tens of thousands of southward migrating Vaux's swifts.

You are accustomed to being the token nature nerd in most crowds, and though you realized that many if not most of those people were there for the spectacle and would not identify as bird watchers, the fact remains: a thousand people went there that day *to watch birds*. You found a bare patch of grass and settled into your camp chair to join them.

There must have been over a thousand swifts up there, hardly a big night for the location but impressive nonetheless. The birds fluttered and dove erratically like bats, calling to each other as they circled, grouping up and then disbursing like smoke. Simultaneous cheering and booing rang out so you focused your binoculars on the chimney just in time to see a peregrine falcon snatch one of the cigar-shaped birds and flap away to a nearby cedar for dinner. You thought about which team you're on—predator or prey—and similar to most sporting events you realized you don't feel strongly one way or the other. Or maybe it's that you feel strongly both ways. You very much wanted the swifts to make it safely in to roost and you very much wanted the peregrine to eat well, to feed her family. You never much liked team sports.

The sun was sinking. Food packed up and put away, children tiring and settling down on blankets with families and friends, the crowd hushing in concentration and expectation. More binoculars raised.

And then, as dusk fell, the swifts spontaneously and mysteriously concentrated from an amorphous cloud into a swirling funneling black tornado. It weaved and wobbled toward the chimney as if one being and the crowd oohed and wowed as if one being. The birds swirled faster, steadier, denser, and then, suddenly, as if pulled by magnets, dropped spiraling into the chimney.

The curtain fell.

The crowd applauded, we cheered, we roared! Hooray for the swifts! Hooray for nature! Hooray for beauty, hooray for mystery!

Hooray for our team!

～

You sat on a wooden bench in the center of a wooden floor with four white walls and five paintings. You'd been through all the rooms, all the various collections: classical realism, impressionism, surrealism, cubism. Folk art, pop art, art nouveau. You didn't know much about any of the isms or the arts, didn't have the language to classify it, judge it, or intelligently discuss it at all, but you did know that you loved *these* paintings. *These* were your favorites.

The longer you sat there the more the colors seemed to seep into your brain, swirling into your blood like the perfect cocktail, the kind that simultaneously stimulates and calms you, makes you feel smarter, more interesting, more beautiful, and completely comfortable in your own skin. Art can do that. Rothko's neat squares of bold color do that to you every time.

The painting that beckoned you loudest flaunted an electric blue background with two thin rectangles of red. You'd always loved the juxtaposition of electric blue—like blue glass—paired with blood red. The discordance hurt your eyes, made them throb and pulse in the most delicious way.

When you finally had to blink you noticed you were not alone in the room; others had gathered there in silence to look at squares of color on the walls. You wondered what they saw. You wondered what Rothko saw. You understood that you could never know that.

You understood the drive to create, to put pen to paper, fingers to clay, or brush to canvas. That visceral need to express some hidden part of you, get it out of you, craft it into what it's crying out to be, and hold it up to the light. What mystified you more, sometimes, was how those creations became almost as distinct lives, capable of reaching out on their own independently of the artists who created them. And we, in that room, we'd come to see *these* creatures. To stare—though our eyes watered and twitched—disciples of art, disciples of human creation.

~

You were devouring The Diary of Anais Nin. You highlighted and underlined, made exclamation points in the margins. At times it was as if she wrote the thoughts from your own mind, except in new ways you hadn't yet articulated. Torn between wanting to experience human culture, the bohemian artists' life, and loving solitude. Needing time alone with a journal to make sense of it all. "My happiness with human beings is so precarious, my confiding moods rare, and the least sign of non-interest is enough to silence me. In the journal I am at ease."[28] Yes, you think. Just like you.

No matter that she wrote of Paris in the 1930s. Through her eyes, her Paris might as well have been Nabokov's St. Petersburg, Patti Smith's New York, your Portland, your Seattle. Human culture. Same team.

You looked up from your book from your window seat and noticed how loud the train was that evening. Tuned in to the different voices, different languages, a shout, a laugh, a song, all of you packed together on that train on that evening in that city. Outside the crows were winging to their evening roost, dozens, hundreds maybe, flapping, diving, gliding, black confetti in the lavender sky. You know they must have been chattering away too, a cawing crowing cacophony. Crow culture.

As the train rumbled onto the bridge over the river, the fading sun glinted amethysts on the water, painted the cottonwoods on the far bank indigo. A solitary great blue heron lifted from the shallows and flapped once, twice, and glided upriver, spindly legs trailing behind. You pressed your forehead against the coolness of the window and watched, alone.

The Great Divide

The morning after the first snowfall in the opalescent light of predawn, I waited for you. Binoculars in my lap, coffee cooling on the porch railing, phone clock glowing 7:01.

At 7:02 there you were, crunching through the aspen grove toward me, binoculars already harnessed on. I jumped to my feet and scampered down the porch steps. As soon as you got close enough to hear, I blurted, *You want to see something cool?*

I'm pretty sure I giggled, and almost took your hand right then. Like a child with her father, or maybe, a teenager with her lover. But we were none of these to each other. Just two almost-strangers in the same place at the same time with a word in common, *naturalist*. You followed me to the edge of the meadow, where I pointed to a large impression in the snow. An animal track, nearly the size of my face.

At my age, in my hermitude, I usually make these discoveries alone. Usually keep them to myself. Or maybe, if I share, if I show, I restrain my excitement. Rein in my glee, protect that tender place so they can't see that these sort of things are not trivial curiosities; these encounters are significant, momentous events. My sense that you might actually feel the same was almost too much to bear.

You did want to see. And maybe it was the morning light reflecting off ice crystals on the crimson and gold of autumn's vestments, but your eyes flickered like firelight. Like a child's eyes, or maybe a teenager's. Once you saw, you crouched down and felt. Placed your fingers lightly at first, then pressed into the impressions left by warm feet not long before. Five fingers into five round toes, so much like our own. The palm of your hand into the arch of a bare foot, creased into lines like our feet—the track so clear a palm reader might decipher a past there, and maybe, a future. You held your hand there, and I imagined you could feel her warmth, somehow, lingering above the snow. When you stood we both looked across the meadow, our eyes following the indigo script written on a two-inch crust of fresh snow, the textbook bigfoot hind prints and half-moon fronts of a black bear.

Up to the recycling bin, knocked over and spilling an empty oil jug, an industrial-sized yogurt container, a wine bottle. Across the meadow adjacent to the lodge, under the apple tree where the snow disappeared, and through the garden in the place where the fence leaned down to the ground too tired after years of mountain snows to remain standing. One direction and then the other, crossing its own tracks, then off through the pines toward the Wenatchee River.

We headed for the river too, to a decommissioned road-turned pedestrian bridge. *Crunch, slush, crunch,* our steps spoke loudly in the softening crust but soon the river roared louder, thick with already melting snow. Clumps sloughed off ponderosa pines, the musky smell of snow and pinesap familiar to you, at home on the arid east slope of the Washington Cascades, but for me the exotic smell of faraway landscapes, of places I pass through but never stay. Nothing like the saccharine sweetness of sugar maple snow from the northeastern coastal forests of my youth, nor the misty cedar perfume of my western Cascades home.

This is where the kinglets were yesterday, I said, pointing to an aspen at the edge of the bridge. And though they weren't there anymore, nor could we hear anything but the river right then, nothing moving around yet in the chill dawn, I could see you imagining them there, a flock of golden-crowned princes flitting about. Watching your smile and the way your eyes crinkled I knew you heard them in your mind too. Those crystal bell hymns sung out on my side of the mountain and yours, so joyous, so jubilant they just might keep the earth turning in winter.

Crossing over to the other side, we did see and hear a few birds, enough to warrant the name birdwalk. Steller's jays scolded someone, probably us, a distant flock of pine siskins zipped among the treetops, and red-breasted nuthatches trumpeted from the dense pine forest with the *No Trespassing* sign. The white tail flash of a dark-eyed junco led us to a crimson hawthorn thicket with a busy mountain chickadee, that black-mohawked mountain ruffian version of its tamer suburban cousin. In the language of birders everywhere, we needed only point, or maybe just stop and aim binoculars somewhere, and the other would take the cue. Our only sounds quiet exclamations, *oh wow*, or *hello there*, or just a hum, a nod, a smile, confirmation that we both got it.

At the top of a lofty ponderosa, one twitching, agitated crow cawed out of synch with its jerky movements like a video soundtrack with a delay. He didn't seem concerned about us directly below, as he looked off in the distance. We watched him in silence for a while, looked where he was looking, shrugged, and moved on. But when we retraced our steps toward the bridge we discovered a potential source of his apprehension—fresh coyote tracks paralleled ours.

All of this would have been enough to return invigorated and enlivened, back to the workshop that brought us together that weekend. Enough to feel content to return to a hot breakfast and a day spent with the others in the wooden-beamed lodge with the crackling fireplace.

But. Back on the bridge, facing upriver toward the North Cascades wilderness, you saw something. *Look!* you blurted, grabbing my arm. I looked. In the distance silver clouds hugged snowy peaks, from which the points of frosty pines twined down to the river's edge. Interspersed with the white-tipped greens were aspen yellows and dogwood reds, newly accented with white pom-poms. All framed the pewter river specked with boulders and ribboned riffles, where I now saw something else moving. Something big was crossing the river.

We knew who we hoped it would be, but in the cautious way of naturalists, we gathered all the evidence. Used what we saw, what we heard, what we almost smelled, and what we sensed beyond all that. Too steady and purposeful for an eddied log. Too big for an otter, or even a coyote. A black mastiff, or newfoundland, maybe? Binoculars up, we were sure. Not a dog, a bear. *Our* bear, was crossing the river.

The river was strong but she was stronger. She made it look easy, seemed almost graceful in her steady progress from west to east. In the river she was no heavy lumbering beast, not splashy and spastic like a dog after a stick but smooth and gliding, more like a giant furred seal, completely at home.

At the midpoint of the river she raised her head higher and looked around, looked back, paddled a little circle, then turned around to return. What was she doing? What was she looking for?

I'm not sure who saw the second one, who grabbed whom or who gasped and who squealed. It didn't matter; by then we didn't need to communicate. I was in your head as you were in mine. Without speaking, without looking at each other, feet on the bridge but all senses telescoping to the same point in the river, we were of one mind.

What we saw was a smaller bear just upriver from where the first had returned. He waded in and started to swim across. A yearling, maybe, or perhaps a mate? Not quite as graceful but focused, determined, the second bear crossed the river from west to east. On the far bank he looked back, and then disappeared into the forest.

We froze, time froze, though the river rushed on.

One bear on each side of the river. It felt wrong. I felt wrong, could physically feel it in my chest. When there was only one bear, bumbling along doing her own thing, it didn't seem much to matter where she went, what she did. But now there were two, and everything had changed. I wanted, I needed them to be together. At my age, in my hermitude, that need confused me.

Of course they didn't need to be together. They were bears. Probably they were even better off on their own, fending for themselves. Everything was fine. I was fine.

But then, that bigger bear splashed back in and set out across the river again. This time, she didn't hesitate. This time, she paddled resolutely to the east side and trundled into the forest at the same place as the first bear. I couldn't see them anymore but I imagined them reuniting. I felt it. I knew they were together.

On the inside I whooped, I cheered, I jumped for joy! On the outside I relaxed. I unclenched. I exhaled and felt something warm and syrupy flow through me from core to fingertips.

Then, I found myself back on the bridge, next to you. It felt strange to be over here, you over there. You smiled, sighed. I smiled, nodded.

I felt… I wanted…what?

I looked away. The morning mist had lifted from the river and the sun had risen into a monochromatic yellow. You noticed too, said something about the light changing, the magic dissipating. I couldn't think of the right thing to say then.

I checked the time. We were going to be late for breakfast.

We hurried off the bridge, through the pines, across the meadow, and back to the lodge, to the rest of the group. *Did you see the bear tracks*, I yelled to others coming up. *Cool*, they said. *We saw the bears*, I said. *Awesome*, they said. You went inside.

At breakfast we sat at the same table but at opposite ends. At a lull in the various conversations about writing, the state of the publishing industry, artist residencies, food allergies, and politics, I managed an awkward smile in your direction that was supposed to mean something though I am not sure what, and I couldn't feel how it landed.

Later, car packed up and remaining snow cleared from my windshield, I walked the riverbank alone. The aging snow had melted and refrozen the once-clear track scripts into gibberish. On the bridge, kinglets chittered. A jay scolded. The gray river was almost still. You were already gone. I returned to the parking lot, got in my car, and crossed back over the mountain to the west side.

Licorice Ferns in Winter

"Go find vole scat" was how the day began, and without question we twelve adults trotted off the gravel parking lot into a feral meadow, wet with a chill December rain. Newer trackers watched the experienced to learn where one might look for the droppings of the plump little rodents, and without speaking we all soon knew that parting the clumps of dead and dying grasses revealed well-used overland tunnels. Vole tunnels, we presumed. Hunched over and crouched or crawling on all fours in the raw wetness amidst encroaching blackberry vines, we scoured the meadow on a treasure hunt for animal sign, because this was a wildlife tracking class and we were the sort who thought this type of thing great fun.

Jackpot! Annika found the first latrine, a somewhat rain-bloated pile of tan scats like mushy Tic Tacs. She scooped them onto a cottonwood leaf and stood to show us all, bright eyes smiling from beneath auburn curls. We *oohed* and *ahhed*, nodded, and studied her treasure before scurrying off to find more. When our instructor Marcus finally pulled us away from the task half an hour later, we'd discovered several more piles and a dozen more tunnels. How many voles lived in that suburban western Washington field? We wondered, discussed, guessed, and moved on to discover who else lived in and around that little patch of wildness.

We traced lines of moss growing in five parallel scars in an alder tree, then five more above that, and again until we realized they were the impressions of a long-ago bear climb. We hypothesized that the similar but tinier lines in a nearby tree were from a baby bear, until measurement and deeper thought turned bear into raccoon. Wondering and discussion transformed large cedar bark scrapes into territorial deer antler rubs, and tiny nibbles on exposed roots of the same tree into Douglas squirrel's calling card. Teaching assistant Adam scratched his beard and pontificated on red-breasted sapsuckers' geometric sapwell designs in a cottonwood. Marcus rested one hand in the pocket of his red hoodie and used the other to outline the animal who had left a large rounded depression in the grass, until we could picture exactly how the blacktail deer had tucked her back legs under her in her pre-dawn bed. Sarah tugged a licorice fern gently from a clump of them growing on a mossy maple and as she nibbled the bittersweet root we observed how lush and verdant these winter-green ferns looked after so much rain. Next we all wondered who would have taken a bite off the end of a thorny blackcap cane dipping groundward nearby. Deer? Aplodontia? Rabbit? Scott found dry round snowshoe hare droppings nearby, and when I discovered the unmistakable soft fur of a lagomorph snagged on one of the thorns we came to a consensus.

It was the sort of dreary Pacific Northwest winter morning I would have been perfectly content inside my quiet home, still in pajamas and nursing my second cup of coffee, but instead I had just spent three hours in a marshy field by a parking lot, and I couldn't have been happier.

To be in company, even with the best, is soon wearisome and dissipating. I love to be alone. I never found the companion that was so companionable as solitude. We are for the most part more lonely when we go abroad among men than when we stay in our chambers.

–Henry David Thoreau[29]

I used to believe that. It sounded so comforting and safe that I wanted to believe it about myself. I filled Acorn Designs lined journals with tiny perfect print using ultra-micro ballpoint pens about my complete self-sufficiency and need of no one. As if writing the words would make them true.

And I tried; I did. I escaped to wilderness repeatedly, even moved there, shunned what little community I had access to and let me tell you, I almost lost my mind. I began to forget how to connect with people, started to grow bitter and occasionally outright mean. I'm lucky I'm not heavily medicated, or dead.

We all have our need for solitude, we sensitive introverts do, and I'm glad I learned how to be content and happy on my own. But alone forever in a mountain-man or desert island sort of way? Not my nature.

~

After lunch we recessed in an adjacent animal-inhabited field with the classic children's game of "don't step on the lava," wherein scattered molehills were the only safe places to stand. For those of us who grew up in the '70s and '80s, lava was the most dangerous ground cover we could imagine.

Just out of college or retired, teacher or administrator or herbalist or engineer, we adult students of life let down our guard, let loose and played. We hopped and leaped, slid and squealed, and oh how we laughed.

Fueled by fun we struck out on the trail, into the forest. We took a cue from Marcus' brisk pace that this was not a wander; he had a destination in mind. Still, we looked around as we walked, looked up and down and paused to point out interesting discoveries before scooting ahead to catch up with the others. A track in the mud—dog or coyote? More stripped cedar bark. Deer or elk? Bell-like tinkling of golden-crowned kinglets thirty feet up in a hemlock. A pile of Douglas fir cone bracts on a rotting stump. We shared a few words here and there, questions and confirmations, but body language spoke louder. We pointed, nodded. Raised eyebrows or shrugged. Breathed in the sweet Pacific Northwest perfume of cedar and fir, moss and lichen, mud and rain. Looked into each others' eyes and smiled, sighed, yawned.

...the only people for me are the mad ones, the ones who are mad to live, mad to talk, mad to be saved, desirous of everything at the same time, the ones who never yawn or say a commonplace thing, but burn, burn, burn like fabulous yellow roman candles exploding like spiders across the stars and in the middle you see the blue centerlight pop and everybody goes "Awww!"

–Jack Kerouac[30]

I used to believe that. It sounded so cool and rebellious that I wanted to believe it about myself. I wrote it in my high school journal in purple ink and decorated the page with stars, the kind I'd practiced over and over so I could draw them without any lines in the middle. As if writing the words would make them true.

And I tried; I did. I befriended, dated, slept with, and attempted to keep up with a lot of mad ones over the years and let me tell you, they are terribly exhausting. Most weren't very nice; some were outright mean. Many of them are medicated now. A few of them are dead.

We all have our mad times, we awake and aware people do, and I'm not advocating somnambulance. But Mr. Kerouac and his mad ones? Not my people.

Marcus abruptly cut off the trail, bushwacking across the forest floor. We followed, fanning out to disburse our impact, over logs and under vine maple arbors. Around head-high cedar stumps topped with salal and red huckleberry, and through clumps of sword fern and Oregon grape. I'd been watching my feet and chatting with Gayle about something or other when I looked up to notice Marcus and the first few behind him had stopped and were standing quietly. We shut up and joined the line looking out at the surprise of open water in the middle of the forest. An ethereal wetland stretched away from us in the mist. Others arrived and went silent, until our whole group stood quietly, just watching, listening, breathing.

The water was so still. At what looked like the midpoint of the pool a mound of sticks suggested the pond's probable engineers, but if they were around they were likely fast asleep. Standing snags, long ago debarked and delimbed so that they more resembled telephone poles, loomed in deep water. If I squinted I could make out several woodpecker-designed cavities of variable sizes that in spring would likely be inhabited by chickadees or nuthatches, wood ducks or screech owls, but were empty for now. Now, the only visible birdlife consisted of a handful of mallards floating on the glassy surface, heads tucked back in slumber. We were still too. Watching. Listening. Breathing.

The gray sky hung low, dipping down into the silver fog, which swirled above the pond and wafted into the forest where we stood rooted for long minutes among naked alders, maples, and cedars. A breeze lifted wood-sweetened raindrops onto our faces and into our hair. We watched. We listened. We breathed.

Finally, Marcus spoke, but just two words. *Thank you*, he said. Thank you.

The only people for me are the wild ones, the ones who are wild to explore, wild to learn and wonder, and wild to play, the ones who know that to speak isn't nearly as important as to look and listen. Wild ones who may chatter like squirrels when excited, but who are equally content to be quiet and watchful like deer. Who know the joy of yawning and relaxing together in the forest like well-fed bears. And most importantly, the ones who understand the sacredness of spontaneous, sustained, communal silence.

To be in their company is to feel supported and nourished, seen and validated. And to remember that solitude, however comfortable, is never so companionable as quality time with your people. People who invigorate each other like gentle rain on thirsty licorice ferns unfurling on mossy maples, so that you can't help but smile and breathe each other in and whisper, again and again, thank you. Thank you.

Lone Wolf

We all had spring fever, the whole lot of us, from twenty-two-year-old young buck to seventy-year-old wise elder. Like feral dogs or cats in heat, our energy was palpable, even visible. Eyes wide and sparking, nostrils flared, mouths open, bodies ready to move. It was bound to happen—our small clan of naturalists plucked from the misty moss-drenched pacific north-wet dreamland we called home and dropped into an arid scrubby meadow of yellow arrowleaf balsamroot, red fritillaries, and bluebells under blazing sun and cobalt sky. Everything was brighter, lighter, as on a new planet with lower gravity. We had space to roam, time to explore, and all our senses yearned to taste the novelty. Where the wildflower meadow ended the conifered hills began, then hills gave way to snow-frosted peaks and when our leader Dave pointed up there as one of our options for the day, that's where we all wanted to go. Had to go. Just try and stop us.

Ruffed grouse drummed as we shoveled in the last of the oatmeal, zipped up tents, filled waterbottles, packed lunches into daypacks, and headed out to see what the landscape might reveal if we paid the right kind of attention. The kind of attention our earth-connected ancestors learned young out of necessity, but which we had sought out as adults through a nine-month wildlife tracking course.

No roads or trails, not even a solid plan, we set out to follow our curiosity, our hunches, our intuition. Through the aspen grove where Hammond's flycatchers and yellow-rumped warblers foraged for freshly hatched insects, crunching cones under our feet in the gently sloping ponderosa pine woodlands where meadowlarks sang from unseen knolls, then the real ascent began. Dave found the easiest path up, around boulders and wiry naked shrubs, avoiding clumps of balsamroot and newly emerging lomatium, and we followed, heads down, like pack mules. We climbed, huffing and panting, removing layers, and we climbed some more.

Where the hillside leveled off before rising again, in a small sheltered grove of firs, we rested. We guzzled water, pulled out apples or handfuls of trail mix, and gazed down on the specks of our tents in the valley, pleased with ourselves. Then looked up at where we intended to go and readied ourselves to continue. Until we noticed Dave and a couple of the more experienced trackers looking at each other, around at the ground, the trees, back at each other, nodding. We'd missed something. After seven months together we were still learning to read the earth, but we had at least become proficient in tracking our human companions.

We looked at each other, around at the ground, the trees, and our mentors. They smiled and said nothing. We looked closer. Got down on hands and knees, crawled around. Sniffed the earth. Pawed at piles of needles and cones and… what's this? Old bones. Deer bones. Kill site. We squinted, looked further. Looked again. A rectangular patch of earth, slight impression, bare of thicker duff, at one time scraped clean. One by one we knew.

I am cougar.

A solitary animal, I spend most of my days alone. Sleeping in a dip of the ridge in the sunshine, sheltered in a rocky crevice from the rain and snow. Wandering by moonlight. I scrape the earth to leave my scent, my writing broadcast on the ground. Sometimes trees. I inhale the writing of my neighbors, the dominant male, juvenile male, and other females of my kind whose territories overlap. I listen for the clucking of grouse, the rustling of gophers, the silence of deer. I listen to the songbird broadcast. I see for miles. I see in the darkness. I sleep, I wander, I survey the mountains and valleys of my home. Solitude is my strength and my solace.

When I'm hungry, I hunt.

Sink my teeth into the warm neck of the deer and hold tight until he stops struggling. Drag him under cover, here, where I can feed in peace. But not necessarily alone. Maybe I share with others of my kind, because they've shared with me. Other lives will be fed too, whether timidly alongside me or later, when I've had my fill—other mammals, birds, insects, fungus, even plants. Because though we are solitary, we are still part of a network, always in relationship. We thrive alone, together.

A white-breasted nuthatch chortled from high up in the fir, and we moved on. Up through firs and lodgepole pines where snow patches in the grass gave way to grass patches in the snow and then just snow, except for melted out circles around the larger trees. The smell of pine needles and dusty soil joined with the metallic smell of old snow.

At the top of the ridge we pulled out lunches or more snacks. Dave and his teaching assistants headed off in opposite directions seeking tracks. The rest of us looked down on the valley, at the green and brown hills encircling it, and then the white peaks beyond. I trained my binoculars on a floating speck in the distance, then another, both circling up slowly, without flapping. Time slowed as I watched the two drift together then apart, growing larger as they rose closer. Only when one *cronk*ed did I recognize they were ravens. Lowering my binoculars I noticed fellow students focusing closer, toward a nearby clump of aspen trees fluttering in motion. Binoculars back up I followed their lead—a flock of mountain bluebirds hawked insects further along the ridge.

Our mentors returned saying they hadn't found much in the way of animal sign, so we agreed to just follow the ridgetop parallel with our valley, exploring on the way, before we dropped back down toward our camp to complete a loop. We continued on.

On level ground then and with our general direction settled, we fanned out a little as we wandered. Those more in the open found deep patches of snow where they sunk up to thighs in some spots, whereas those who stuck to the clumps of trees found shallower snow iced over into peaks and dips that looked like waves. A little slippery but you could walk on top there so I chose that path.

Stalking mysterious bird calls I moved quicker than the others, listening and looking ahead instead of looking down and around—ever a birder, even in a tracking class. I did stop to investigate whenever I spotted a rounded impression in the snow, despite the fact that those tracks were often left by snow itself, clumped and blown down from trees above. Our brains seek patterns and order where there may be none.

I spied one such impression off by itself, hardened into the crust out in the open. I didn't expect much. I skittered over to it on the ice, and peered down. It was an old track, frozen down a couple inches and partially filled in with loose snow, once soft but now crystallized. And yet I could clearly recognize that this was not just a snow clump. This impression, about four inches across and four inches long, had clear indents of four toes and claws, and a larger footpad. An animal had been here. A mammal. A carnivore.

I tried not to get overly excited as I called the group over and asked what they thought. After looking around and carefully confirming that this was the only track in the immediate vicinity—likely the one place the snow had been softer at one point so the animal punched through the crust—we gathered around and conferred. First with vague *hmmming*, head tilting and book consulting, then open discussion. We knew who we hoped it would be, despite the fact that our hope was an animal that we didn't think was there anymore. It was historically there before human persecution and eradication, then back for a while, then more human persecution and eradication, and now only a rumor, a Grimm fairy tale.

The track was so weathered, melted out and filled in, even the expert trackers among us were hesitant to say for sure, but with Dave's agreement we decided it was probably a cougar track. More rounded than oblong, larger impression of the footpad, and not unusual to show claw marks in deep snow. We already knew cougars lived in the area. All things considered, it was the most likely explanation. Cougar track. That was exciting. Would normally have been exciting. I tried to be excited. We moved on, not saying it out loud, but scanning the ground more carefully now. Looking for something else. Someone else.

We all got into our tracker bodies then. I put my binoculars away and stepped lightly, scanning down and ahead, alternating between focusing closely and relaxing into the wide-angle softer gaze that sometimes allows you to see differently, more. I saw pine needles frozen into crust. Entrances to tunnels used by montane voles to scurry under the snow. Frozen waves and troughs, hills and valleys in the black-flecked white. Bare patches of needles and mud. But no tracks, human or animal.

Until, *over here*, Adam called. We came. He was standing in a denser section of lodgepole forest where a only a ribbon of snow remained. And on top of that snow, pixelated in mud, the most perfect, textbook canine tracks. One after another, the giant tracks of a four-toed, sharp-clawed animal who'd trotted along right where we were standing. In a place where no people had walked, far from anywhere a dog might roam. And we knew.

I am lone wolf.

I am a social animal striking out alone. The odd one out, an exception to the rule. I've left behind the protection of my pack, but also their aggression. The confines of a rigid social structure, all the rules, the narrow spaces I never fit. I am learning to be independent, to hunt alone, feed alone, sleep alone, and for that I am stronger, if a little neurotic. And I am free. I am becoming an individuated self, an *I am* more solid than members of a pack may ever know. My experiences, my perspective, my thoughts are mine and mine alone.

I am an explorer, a wanderer, an opportunist. I might roam hundreds of miles from where I was born, river valleys to mountain tops, dense forest to arid scrublands. Sniff out water sources to quench my thirst and meaty morsels to satisfy my hunger. Use my powerful jaws to grasp and hold, tear and chew. Without strength in numbers to hunt larger prey like deer and elk I make do with jackrabbit and pocket gopher, beaver and muskrat, grouse and vole. I will scavenge the leavings of a cougar kill. And yes, if I stray close enough to a ranch I might help myself to one of the slow, witless farm animals you left unprotected. But I am not the big bad wolf. I will not huff and puff and blow your house down, or eat your grandmother. I am also not a terrorist, and will not indiscriminately massacre my own kind as domestic humans do in my name.

I am definitely not, nor will I ever be, your pet. You will never make me sit or stay. I will not come when you call, nor will I cower at your feet. I am the essence of wildness, free in all the ways that you are not. And that, I know, is why you still feel so threatened by me.

But maybe, after years of wandering, of sleeping alone in forested hollows or abandoned badger dens, of slinking around the edges of other packs, of howling at the moon and only hearing the echo of my own voice against the ridges—maybe, one time, another of my kind might howl back. Then another. And eventually, I might find myself part of a chorus of voices far more beautiful than any single voice could ever be. After a while perhaps I'll be accepted into a new pack, learn their ways and find their social structures acceptable, even nourishing. I'll remember the comforts of companionship, the levity of play, and best of all, the deep satisfaction of being truly heard and seen by my own kind. And just maybe, one day after that, I'll even find myself rediscovering the ecstatic peace of curling up next to a warm sighing mate, limbs intertwined.

We took measurements and pictures, sketches and notes, attempting to soak up as much wolfiness as possible and loathe to leave that spot, that proof of primal wildness still among us, or rather, among us again. Only when Dave asked, *where is he now*, did we look up and ahead, remember, yes, he's still out there, please let him be out there. We packed up and moved on, noses pointed down, ears open, searching. Searching. But we found nothing more.

After roaming along the ridge for a while we came to a point where we looked down on our camp far below and decided we best start heading down. Out of the snow and into the wildflowers, sunny clumps of arrowleaf balsamroot among the sagey green scrub and rocky soil. We zigzagged down to minimize the slope but still, it was steep.

A pile of slate-gray feathers indicated a sooty grouse kill and we picked over it eagerly, hoping for evidence of wolf or maybe cougar but it soon became clear that the feathers had been plucked, not torn or sheared. Likely a bird kill. Perhaps the great-horned owl who'd serenaded us at night.

The valley seemed to stretch away from us and what had seemed a simple descent turned into multiple smaller hills and valleys. When we came to a shaded Doug fir grove with dappled sunlight where rabbit and deer pellets indicated it was a popular resting spot, we took their cue and lay in the grass. Coming down from the adrenaline of cougar and wolf sign, tired climbing muscles setting in, lazy afternoon energy setting in and still a ways from the valley below, we settled into dazed lounging. Flat on the dry earth, heads on backpacks, baseball caps pulled down over eyes. The final jabber trailed off into silence. A sooty grouse called from the hills above, ruffed grouse drummed from the valley below, and silence.

And then, from just beyond the firs, an animal sound I didn't recognize. Like the sporadic squeak of a rusty wheelbarrow, subtle and irregular. I popped up and looked around. Looked at the group—all still snoozing. I, however, couldn't ignore it. It sounded again—*eek-eek*. I stood, grabbed my binoculars, and headed off in search of the mystery.

The call had come from up high, not ground level, so that narrowed my search area significantly. Beyond the firs, beyond and above the few scrubby shrubs, one giant ponderosa pine towered above us all. I put up my binoculars and scanned. Circled the pine and scanned some more. The animal had stopped calling but I thought I heard a cracking crunching sound, a feeding sound, from up high. Perhaps a squirrel?

Then I saw him. Inching up and around the flakey bark, probing in crevices, flicking off loose patches. Not a squirrel, a bird. Black body, pure white head except for the small patch of red at the back. A white-headed woodpecker! He hopped over to an unopened pine cone and went to work on it from below, jabbing and prying at it to get at the seeds. I scanned the rest of the tree and didn't see any others, just that one flash of black and white and the sounds of his foraging.

White-headed woodpecker was a rare bird, even for eastside locals, so I looked back toward my lazing tribe, then back up, unsure of whether to interrupt their reverie to call them over to see. In my hesitation the bird flew on, leaving me standing alone next to the tree.

I looked at the pine. Up at stout branches that circled up and up to the sky, and thick red flakes of bark on a trunk I couldn't reach around. I leaned in, forehead against trunk, and smelled that faint vanilla ponderosa smell just waking up in the warmth of spring. Looked down and saw the earth under this one tree's canopy carpeted with bluebells and shoots of green grass where just beyond was still brown and dead. And I knew.

I am wolf tree. That curious human name for a tree who grows apart from other trees, free to branch out in multiple directions, not thin and cramped in the crowd. In the forest I might have withered and died young, but out in the open field with the sun on my skin and wind in my hair I grew strong and self-sufficient. I learned to tend to my own needs. I took up space and protected it with my elbows out. Separate from my own kind, I have thrived.

Of course, I was never truly alone. I've always had the birds—woodpeckers spiraling up, drumming, nuthatches spiraling down, giggling, and meadowlarks tucked away singing so that their songs seem to come from everywhere and nowhere. The taller and stronger I grew the better I've been able to shelter other lives. I'm the signpost for scraping bobcats and scatting coyotes. I shelter cougar as she takes her dinner, and babysit baby bears while their mom sniffs out berries. Perhaps one day I'll even shelter the wolf pack who will move back, if you let them.

And maybe, now, I am ready to reach out and invite the whole forest back in. Not just the sprouts who grow at my feet but the complete richness of diverse communities, of other trees like me and different from me too. Let all the wild back in and cherish the complexity of all my relations. Learn to share more of myself, let my guard down, and adapt to a different way of being. I'll learn to be of service, to be an elder truly.

Maybe it will kill me. Eventually, it will. Whether I'm shaded out or eaten up or just used up. But even then, especially then, life will continue from my broken body, from the fecund earth I leave behind. And finally, I will understand that separation was always an illusion. Death will dissolve any remaining *I am*, until all that's left is *We are*.

I returned to the group as they stirred and stretched, and we readied ourselves for the final descent back into camp. Energized by our break and perhaps thinking ahead to hot food and other comforts awaiting below, we trotted and bounded down the open hillside, careful to avoid multiplying clumps of yellow balsamroot. We'd gotten fairly spread out when we noticed Dave, at the lead, stopped and facing the knoll ahead. A group of deer stood there, watching us, ears twitching nervously. A few had already started pointing themselves away from us, necks craned around to keep an eye on us as we approached.

Without speaking we all slowed to a gentle walk. Turned our bodies to the side and made wide arcs away from the deer.

Only when we'd circled around and they resumed heads-down grazing did we resume our final frolicking descent into camp.

Vesper sparrows sang in the early evening as we each attended to our own needs. Some joined together to cook dinner over camp stoves, joking and laughing. Others of us sat alone, following the final sunlit patches along the meadow, consulting field guides, drawing tracks and sign seen earlier that day, or writing in journals. Two started the process of building a fire; one chopped wood while another set up a kindling pyramid in the fire pit.

One by one we made our way over to the fire pit, helping by carving smaller kindling pieces off the bigger logs or shaving bits of cedar bark into a soft tinder bundle, or sitting back on the wooden benches chatting. Scott, a young man with a flair for friction fire, readied his home-made kit and began the process of bowing cedar spindle on cedar plank. One by one we hushed, watching. Scott knew his technique but he was rusty, hadn't prepped the notch in his fire board quite right so for long minutes wood screeched on wood but no ember.

Emily started a song we'd learned earlier in the year, a song written by a former student of the wilderness school, and we joined her. As the songbirds quieted, an owl *hooooed*, and the stars blinked on, we raised our voices in harmony. The chorus—*I am I am*. A whiff of cedar smoke, the dim glow of a coal, and with human breath, spark into flame. I looked around at the faces lit up in the sudden glow, and I knew.

I am a human animal. No matter how solitary, no matter how wild, I will always possess a longing for and deep satisfaction in communing with my clan. Going feral I found my way through fire, water, earth, and sky. Among cottonwood, cedar, maple, and pine. Alongside horse, hummingbird, raven, and owl. Otter, deer, rabbit, and bear. Cougar, wolf, and wolf tree. But ultimately and always, back to myself, and my people.

First the kindling caught and then the bigger logs, and soon the fire was crackling. For long minutes we watched it in silence, together. In our circle of light the rest of the world seemed to fade away but we hadn't forgotten it; we held it in our minds and our bodies. One by one, we began to tell our stories.

Fairy Tale

What do you want to be when you die? This is the logical extension of the question my generation was asked ad nauseam, our parents still believing in the American Dream, that all we had to do was study and get good grades and graduate good schools and we could grow up to do, be, whomever we wanted. I hear that still works for some. Those with the right combination of privilege and money and luck and the right gender and skin color and social skills and mental fortitude and dreams contained in the grade school guidance counselor's list of career choices like doctor lawyer businessman insurance administrator politician, maybe they can grow up to be exactly whom they want to be.

The rest of us, we do what we need to for work, hopefully something that doesn't make us crazy or broken or dead which means we're luckier than many. And if we get to do what we want and be whom we want at other times, even little snatches of time, then usually, it's enough. Five a.m. candlelit darkness with coffee cooling on the coaster, wrapped in a blanket by the radiator, scrawling in a journal with a favorite pen. Lunch break wander away from fluorescent lights and the glow of spreadsheets on double computer monitors, out into the real sunlight down to the cottonwoods by the river, binoculars in hand. Twilight jog through the cedar forest, along the devil's club swamp where barred owls call from the bigleaf maple and maybe, even hopefully, a cougar watches from the shadows. Birdwalks, plantwalks, and tracking walks with others who seek to notice and teach and learn the world around them. Solo wanders to learn from mountain, desert, river or sea. Storytelling and listening, making music, crafting art, creating something beautiful. Or ugly, as long as it's true. In between times, in between places, in so many ways I grew up to be exactly whom I wanted to be.

But. After I die? I'm out of here.

Out of the cage of this human body with all its trappings and baggage, its rules and restrictions. Out of here, and into the body of American dipper. That's water ouzel to you country folk. Because of course I'll want to fly—you guessed that—but I also want to swim. To dive into icy creeks to look beneath the water, then come up dancing on rounded stones. To wing up to the top of a cedar tree to see where the river came from, and see where it goes. Then back down, underwater to see within, chiming my liquid tune.

When I tire of that busy life of diving, dancing, singing, and flying, of looking above and below and fore and aft, I will settle down and become a barred owl. Talons curved around the smooth bark of a cedar limb I'll stand, and stay. Doze in the sun and wake in the moonlight. I'll see all—fleas jumping on coyote's fur, fluttering feathers above hummingbird's racing heart, dewdrop on devil's club thorn. I'll hear what goes unseen—licorice fern unfurling in the rain, air bubbles escaping from underneath dipper's wings as she dives, meadow vole gnawing on a cedar rootlet.

On hazy late-summer evenings while the robins are still at vespers I'll call out. In the crystalline winter darkness of the new moon I'll call out. When cottonwood resin turns sleeping buds orange and chorus frogs croak in the cold rain dreaming of spring, I'll hoot and howl and caterwaul. But mostly, I'll remain silent.

I could be the owl for many lives, I think, without tiring of that body. But if I craved more silence, more stillness, I'd root down and become a western redcedar. Then reach up and grow toward the light. I'll sway with the wind, consume sun and soil and sip the rain, donned in lichen necklaces and sword fern skirts. I'll be nibbled by insects and gnawed by deer; I'll host whole universes of miniscule lives on a single branch—food, shelter, home and hideaway. I'll delight in the grip of scaly toes closing around a branch, tickly claws pressing in, a caress of feathers against my roughest parts, the breezy whisper of lift-off, and best of all, ethereal melodies chorusing all around me every dawn.

After a thousand years, perhaps, I'll be ready to think again. To regain the special awareness of human, to wonder and ponder and speculate and contemplate as only we do. But not necessarily bound in a body. Not yet. I will slip out of wood and bark and rise with the fog, walk into the mist. Join the other disembodied ones dwelling there—ghost, spirit, elf, nymph, fairy—whatever name your ancestors or eccentric Aunt Alice might call me.

Untethered, I will dwell in the woodlands. Shimmy in that single cottonwood leaf on an otherwise windless day. Flash like a scarlet flame on a hummingbird's throat in a sunbeam. Glisten in the raindrop on the devil's club thorn. Snuggle coyote pups in the earthen hollow beneath the fallen fir.

Part of me is there already, always has been. Have you seen my shadow in the dappled sunlight on the forest floor? Heard me in the spiraling song of the thrush? Smelled me on the morning dew in the wildflower meadow? Felt me in the waterfall mist on your face, and tasted me on your lips? I am there. I am.

Remember? You are too.

ACKNOWLEDGMENTS

I am grateful to the editors of the following publications, in which earlier versions or excerpts of these essays first appeared: "The Fall" published as "Two Peas" in *Minerva Rising*, "Farm Animals" in *Proximity Magazine*, "Baptisms" in *Portland Review*, "Ablaze" in *Voicecatcher* and in *Voicecatcher*'s Ten Year Anthology: *She Holds the Face of the World*, "Free Hands" in *Masque & Spectacle*, "Them" in *Pilgrimage Magazine*, "Alone Together" in *Timberline Review*, and "Dismembering" as a web exclusive in *Orion Magazine*.

Thank you to all the human communities who helped bring *Wolf Tree* into the world. To writing mentors Ana Maria Spagna, Larry Cheek, David Oates, and fellow students in Northwest Institute of Literary Arts workshops who helped me hone some of these essays and gave me the tools to craft the others. To fellow staff, students, and elders at Wilderness Awareness School for empowering and nurturing holistic interconnections among nature, community, and self. You truly are my people. To visionary editor/publisher Leslie Browning and Homebound Publications for believing in my work and welcoming me into your amazing troupe of contemplative authors. And to my family for your ongoing encouragement and support. Thank you for being you and for letting me be me.

Deep gratitude to the plants, animals, landscapes and elements who nourished, mentored, comforted, and inspired me on this path. Fire and water. New England farms, woodlands, lakes, and islands. Pacific Northwest river valleys, forests, coast, and mountains. Maple, cedar, pine, fir. Raven, barred owl, hummingbird, jay. Horse, black bear, rabbit, raccoon. You are my people too.

NOTES

1   Taylor, James. "You've Got a Friend." *Mud Slide Slim and the Blue Horizon*, Warner Brothers, 1971. Song originally by Carol King from *Tapestry*, A&M, 1971.

2   Silverstein, Shel. *The Giving Tree*. New York: Harper & Row, 1964.

3   Buscaglia, Leo. *The Fall of Freddie the Leaf*. New York: Henry Holt & Co., 1982.

4   Sparks, Randy. "Today." New York: Miller Music Corp., 1964.

5   Baez, Joan. "Dona." *Joan Baez*, Vanguard, 1960. Yiddish folk song originally by Sholom Secunda & Aaron Zeitlin, 1941.

6   American folk song, origin unknown.

7   Mead, M. Nathaniel. "Benefits of Sunlight: A Bright Spot for Human Health" *Environmental Health Perspectives*. 2008 Apr; 116(4): A160–A167. PMCID: PMC2290997. Accessed 2, November 2019. Web. https://www.ncbi.nlm.nih.gov/pmc/articles/PMC2290997/

8   Williams, Terry Tempest. "Ode to Slowness." *Red: Passion and Patience in the Desert*. New York: Vintage Books, 2001. p. 144. Print.

9   Rochat, Philippe. "Five levels of self-awareness as they unfold early in life." *Consciousness and Cognition* 12 (2003) 717-731: p. 728. Downloaded from sciencedirect.com. Web.

10   Vega, Suzanne. "Solitude Standing." *Solitude Standing*, A&M Records, 1987.

11   Hersh, Kristin. "Mississippi Kite." From *Crooked*, an essay collection to accompany the album of the same name. Kristin Hersh, 2010.

12   Merton, Thomas. *The Seven Storey Mountain*. San Diego: Harcourt, 1948. p. 454. Print.

13   Cain, Susan. *Quiet: The Power of Introverts in a World that Can't Stop Talking*. New York: Crown Publishing Group, 2012. p. 237. Print.

14   Dandelion, Ben Pink. "The Difference Between Quaker Meeting and other Services." *Quakerspeak*. Accessed 2 November, 2019. Web. https://quakerspeak.com/difference-between-quaker-meeting-other-christian-services/

15   Whitman, Walt. "Song of Myself." Accessed 2 November, 2019. Web. https://www.poetryfoundation.org/poems/45477/song-of-myself-1892-version

16   Young, Jon. *What the Robin Knows*. New York: Houghton Mifflin Harcourt, 2012. p. 86. Print.

17   ibid. p. 170.

18   King, Barbara. "We May Have Snakes To Thank For Our Acute Vision." *NPR Cosmos & Culture*. 13.7, March 19, 2015. Accessed 2 November, 2019. Web. http://www.npr.org/sections/13.7/2015/03/19/394099609/we-may-have-snakes-to-thank-for-our-acute-vision

19   Young, Jon. *What the Robin Knows*. New York: Houghton Mifflin Harcourt, 2012. p. 163

20   Berger, John. "Why Look at Animals." *About Looking.* New York: Pantheon Books, 1980. Print.

21   Dillard, Annie. "Living Like Weasels." *Teaching a Stone to Talk.* New York: HarperCollins Publishers, 1982. p. 29. Print.

22   Potter, Beatrix. *The Tale of Peter Rabbit.* London: Frederick Warne & Co.,1902 Accessed 2 November, 2019. Web. http://digital.lib.uiowa.edu/peterrabbit/pageflip.html

23   Neely, Nick. "Why Write About Animals." *Essay Daily.* October 29, 2015. Accessed 2 November, 2019. Web. http://www.essaydaily.org/2015/10/why-write-about-animals.html

24   Snyder, Gary. "The Woman Who Married a Bear." *The Practice of the Wild.* New York: North Point Press, 1990. p. 162-164. Print.

25   Haupt, Lyanda Lynn. *Mozart's Starling.* New York: Little, Brown, 2017. p. 209. Print.

26   Doyle, Brian. *Martin Marten.* New York: St. Martins Press, 2015 p. 55. Print.

27   Abram, David. *Becoming Animal.* New York: Pantheon Books, 2010. Print.

28   Nin, Anais. *The Diary of Anais Nin, Volume One: 1931-1934.* New York: The Swallow Press, 1966. p. 224. Print.

29   Thoreau, Henry David. "Solitude." *Walden.* Boston: Ticknor & Fields, 1854. Print.

30   Kerouac, Jack. *On the Road.* New York: Viking Press, 1957. Print.

About the Author

Heather Durham grew up in New England, wandered widely, and now finds herself rooting firmly in the land of ravens and salmon, amidst the towering cedars and moody mists of the Pacific Northwest. She holds a bachelor of arts in psychology from the University of Virginia, a master of science in environmental biology from Antioch New England University, and a master of fine arts in creative nonfiction from the Northwest Institute of Literary Arts. Her essays have been published in a variety of literary journals and her first book, *Going Feral: Field Notes on Wonder and Wanderlust*, was named a Next Generation Indie Book Awards Finalist in Nature writing.

After holding a variety of environmental jobs around the country from park ranger to restoration ecologist, field biologist to naturalist, Heather currently works behind the scenes at Wilderness Awareness School in the foothills of the Washington Cascades. When not working or writing, you are likely to find Heather reading other nature writers or wandering in a riverside cedar grove with a journal, field guide, and binoculars, hunting birdsong.

Learn more at heatherdurhamauthor.com.

HOMEBOUND PUBLICATIONS

We are an award-winning independent publisher founded in 2011 striving to ensure that the mainstream is not the only stream. More than a company, we are a community of writers and readers exploring the larger questions we face as a global village. It is our intention to preserve contemplative storytelling. We publish full-length introspective works of creative non-fiction, literary fiction, and poetry.

WWW.HOMEBOUNDPUBLICATIONS.COM

CPSIA information can be obtained
at www.ICGtesting.com
Printed in the USA
JSHW021535280122
22315JS00002B/4